# Digital Game Culture in Korea

# Digital Game Culture in Korea

## The Social at Play

Florence M. Chee

LEXINGTON BOOKS
*Lanham • Boulder • New York • London*

Published by Lexington Books
An imprint of The Rowman & Littlefield Publishing Group, Inc.

4501 Forbes Boulevard, Suite 200, Lanham, Maryland 20706
www.rowman.com

86-90 Paul Street, London EC2A 4NE, United Kingdom

Copyright © 2023 by The Rowman & Littlefield Publishing Group, Inc.

*All rights reserved.* No part of this book may be reproduced in any form or by any electronic or mechanical means, including information storage and retrieval systems, without written permission from the publisher, except by a reviewer who may quote passages in a review.

British Library Cataloguing in Publication Information Available

**Library of Congress Cataloging-in-Publication Data**

Names: Chee, Florence M., 1979– author. Title: Digital game culture in Korea : the social at play / Florence M. Chee.
Description: Lanham : Lexington Books, 2023. | Includes bibliographical references and index. | Summary: "Focusing on Korea's sociohistorical and technocultural context, this work celebrates and recognizes the foundational role of Korean game culture in shaping global games and play"—Provided by publisher.
Identifiers: LCCN 2023004330 (print) | LCCN 2023004331 (ebook) | ISBN 9781793601391 (cloth) | ISBN 9781793601407 (epub)
Subjects: LCSH: Video games—Social aspects—Korea. | Computer games—Social aspects—Korea. | Video game addiction—Korea. | Video games industry—Korea.
Classification: LCC GV1469.34.S52 C44 2023  (print) | LCC GV1469.34.S52 (ebook) | DDC 794.8—dc23/eng/20230207
LC record available at https://lccn.loc.gov/2023004330
LC ebook record available at https://lccn.loc.gov/2023004331

*For Morgan*

# Contents

| | |
|---|---|
| Preface | ix |
| Acknowledgments | xi |
| Chapter 1: Games as Communication: Savior or Scourge? | 1 |
| Chapter 2: The Rise of Digital Game Culture in Korea | 25 |
| Chapter 3: The Social Addict: Infrastructures of Togetherness | 53 |
| Chapter 4: Gender Pipelines and Pipe Dreams: Games Industry and Mobility | 79 |
| Chapter 5: Gaming the Future: Holding Space for Better Worlds | 101 |
| Bibliography | 109 |
| Index | 119 |
| About the Author | 123 |

# Preface

As of the 2023 publication of this book, it is fitting that its launch coincides with the 25th anniversary of Blizzard Entertainment's StarCraft (1998), and NCSoft's Lineage (1998): games that figure prominently in the online game history of Korea, global eSports, and notably, the research for this monograph, *Digital Game Culture in Korea: The Social at Play*. In South Korea, online games are a prominent part of popular culture and this medium has come under public criticism for various societal ills, such as Internet addiction and a hopeless dependence upon online games.

All too often, studies of engagement with technology reduce questions to their basic variables and social aspects are omitted in the name of science. In terms of addiction to games, I believe addiction is a social construct that does more harm than good when used as biomedical shorthand to describe what is actually a very social means of communication and engagement in community. It is from this point that I began this work in earnest around 2002. This book explores the place and meaning-making practices of online games in everyday life.

This book covers an expanse of time that spans almost twenty years by the time of publication. A perspective that is almost half my life, this book is a necessary touchstone given the research that I have undertaken and collaborated on in the intervening period. The consistent thread was a focus on ethnographic studies of online gaming culture, the fieldwork for which has taken place in numerous settings since 2002. It adds to the body of humanistic accounts concerning Information-Communication Technology (ICT) usage. Given the relatively niche nature of these accounts, they continue to share a marginal status while the power of automated data collection processes gamify and pervade our spaces of play.

Research on the subject of games, play, community, and gamers is by no means exempt or immune to the imperatives of funding and culture wars.

Exactly how has it come to pass, that online games have come to occupy such a prominent place in the media ecology in South Korea, and yet not been replicated in other national contexts? This investigation shows why games are social and the many ways people form community in a game ecosystem through their navigation of everyday life, culture, and meaning. This book argues that though appearances may be deceiving, and gamers often appear solitary and isolated, they are instead lifelines to the social. In this composite sketch of game culture and its attendant practices, I show how rather than addiction at work, it is the social at play.

## STRUCTURE OF THE BOOK

The first chapter discusses addiction as it pertains to online games and suggests some scholarly support for the viewpoint that the rhetoric surrounding a biomedical interpretation of online game addiction may not be the most appropriate way to address problems that have been typically laid at the feet of online gaming (or any other new form of media). The section transitions into discussing my rationale for approaching South Korea as a fieldsite, the approach, and how this examination of online games is a particularly illustrative case of the profound role played by culture, social structure, infrastructure, and policy in audience reception. The second chapter, on the rise of Korean gaming, delves into the foundational aspects of Korean social history and culture that, I assert, set the stage for the present new media scene in South Korea.

The third chapter explores what games mean in the lives of Korean youth according to the ethnographic data I have been collecting during research stays from 2004–2016, having analyzed the emergent practices involved in online game activity. The fourth chapter expands my work with an analysis of the gender dynamics of the games industry coupled with a critical analysis of the Korean games industry and the role it has to play in the upward mobility of young Koreans. The fifth chapter discusses the future of the games industry and implications for design and building a better world. Overall, this book examines the contextual factors of South Korea, in which a medium of communication can begin to be understood within the porous boundaries of its national circumstances and sociotechnical transformation.

# Acknowledgments

It takes a (global) village. I would like to express my gratitude to those who have encouraged and supported this work coming to fruition in the years since the writing of my doctoral dissertation. This work, like its subject matter, is a clear example of the social at play, as it owes much to those who forged paths before me, and continue to do the work for our collective future in academia, industry, and government. Know that my heartfelt gratitude and appreciation extends to you. Thank you to those who have supported me personally and professionally at individual and organizational levels.

To the amazingly kind and generous people with whom I have shared dialogue, insights, and meals—and many of whom persist as friends and colleagues through literally decades—you continue to honor me through long memories and shared history. You are in this book.

In addition to the challenges of functioning during an ongoing global pandemic, I am thankful to those who kept the faith while the world brought us to our collective knees in various ways. Thank you for your recognition and conviviality.

To the editorial team at Lexington Books, especially Nicolette Amstutz, Jessica Tepper, and Deja Ryland, for their continuing support and belief in the work, along with the anonymous reviewers for their positive feedback—thank you for your instrumental role in publishing this book and getting it into the hands of readers.

This book benefits from the ideas, engagement, and collaborations from my lifetime academic community of multidisciplinary researchers represented in the membership rosters of professional organizations such as the Digital Games Research Association, Association of Internet Researchers, International Communication Association, Canadian Communication Association, National Communication Association, International Association for Media and Communication Research, Association for Asian Studies, Association for Computing Machinery, and more. I hope this work contributes well to the continuing pursuit of knowledge in these areas.

I am grateful to worldwide institutional networks, who have been crucial for both intellectual and material support of growing partnerships and collaborations in this communication endeavor. These include invitations to give talks and workshop the concepts in this book through initiatives funded by the National Science Foundation, Social Sciences and Humanities Research Council, Academy of Korean Studies, Korea Foundation, Academy of Finland, University of Jyväskylä, Tampere University, Brown University, University of Pennsylvania, University of Hawaii, Simon Fraser University, and my home base of Loyola University Chicago.

To my family of Canadians, including my chosen family around the globe: you are also in this book. You have shown me that sometimes love is the only condition one needs to get through adversity. Andrea Warner, who told me to just write the acknowledgments and cry through it. Carlos Hernandez Fisher, for your editing, especially helping me watch those US/Canadian spellings. Meera Nair, Richard Smith, Geoffrey Rockwell, and Stuart Poyntz, for always answering my calls from anywhere in the world.

Tom, whose life partnership is a big "reason to be." You have shown true love to manifest through word and deed in these same decades. Thank you for being my partner through all these quest chains and laughing with me during the sweetest reverse ganks.

Most of all, this book is dedicated to Morgan, whose existence has expanded my capacity to find joy and nuance in life's playful moments. Your little face has kept me going through good times and bad. You've made me a better fighter, and my love for you knows no bounds.

—With love from Chicago

*Chapter 1*

# Games as Communication

*Savior or Scourge?*

*This pink eye situation has caused me to hit a new low in my life and general physical/mental health here. After dinner I lay in bed behind the closed door of my room.*

*. . . I wasn't in the mindset to do work. I curled up on my mattress, facing the wall I had gotten to know so well over the last few months, making slight indentations in the grooves with my fingernails . . . slowly . . . precisely. It was then that I realized that the way I had dealt with mental isolation my whole time here was to immerse myself in work. No wonder I was at my wits' end. It wasn't until this sickness affected my vision and work at the computer, that I truly realized how woefully consuming and (sight) work-oriented my life here has been. What made it worse, was that I was in this situation because I had signed up for this whole fieldwork "thing" myself . . .*

*I found myself envious of my husband back in Vancouver who was sleeping in our comfortable bed right now, oblivious to my lone ethnographic angst. It was only 8:15pm for me here in Seoul. Maybe I would go for a walk or something. Then the thought of walking in my district . . . on a cold dark night . . . alone . . . in the dark industrial surroundings . . . turned my stomach. If my friends could see me in this technological paradise now, both eyes matted half shut, pollution-induced bronchitis . . .*

*My fetal position continued for at least another five minutes, with only my own neurotic thoughts to keep me entertained. I thought to myself, "Gee . . . this is really it, isn't it? I'm defined by my work here. There's nothing else to me. If I can't work on it, I don't do it. I don't have real friends here, I'm an ugly red-eyed alien, and I suck." I had hit my final low of suck-ti-tude. How had my glorious cross-cultural expedition come to this? My life was a sitcom, starring a crazy foreigner (me).*

*I took my mobile phone in hand and just held it for a while. I looked at the plastic Stitch character head that was left dangling on the phone (the body had broken off days ago, leaving only a head). Pathetic. I inspected the different curves, textures, colours, and scratches that were on it. Finally, I text messaged Sang one word: "bored."*

*Not long after, I received a reply, "So, what do you want to do?"*

*Alone in my room, but not truly alone, I realized that this device was my link to the outside world . . .*

The preceding text was a series of excerpts from my personal field diary, written while conducting my first fieldwork in Korea during 2004. It was a relatively coherent sliver of my darkest, most undiplomatic thoughts at the time, with most of the topics and their related issues raised in this one day never explicitly making it into subsequent publications concerning online games, culture, social structure, and infrastructure. In comparison, the resultant ethnography one reads here ends up becoming a highly sanitized, qualitative study examining the motivations of Korean youth with their participation in online game communities that might have been more reminiscent of scientific Malinowski (1964) than candid Malinowski (1967), for example.

Reflecting on this work years at a time, I find myself an archaeologist in my own work, reckoning with the affordances and limitations of ethnography as one way of communicating culture. Teaching students for years now, in what I have come to regard as an essential item in a methodological toolkit, I am more forgiving. It is the imperfection and struggle that creates life on the page, standing to change hearts and minds. The vulnerable, playful, and what I, at times, thought were the silliest moments have often been the most memorable. Those impactful moments were the ones quoted back to me by graduate students at academic conferences. I see those graduate students as tenured professors and forces in their respective vocations now. It is in this spirit that this chapter includes the interweaving of various research methodologies, my personal and sustained engagement with people and places, and how this approach shaped the contours of this book.

My concern with the discourse surrounding addiction to online games emerged while studying Sony Online Entertainment's popular massively-multiplayer online role-playing game (MMORPG) EverQuest more than twenty years ago, fueled by my own experiences as a lifelong gamer, and bolstered by a budding community of scholarly game researchers. In our study "Is Electronic Community an Addictive Substance?" (Chee & Smith, 2003) I had the privilege of interviewing folks for whom the game served as what Marshall McLuhan called a therapeutic "counter-irritant" for the trials and travails of everyday life (McLuhan, 1994).

While the game had been thoroughly criticized in the media for allegedly being the instigator of serious social ailments, causing suicides and truancy, this interviewee made a particularly striking statement: "EverQuest saved my life." All the while, with various politicians, lawyers, psychiatrists, and members of the public calling for the labeling of this and other online games as a "harmful/addictive substance," the discourse seemed to favor regulation more befitting that of pharmaceutical narcotics. In contrast to the view of "problematic use" associated with gameplay, the narrative my informant was providing seemed to point at how he used the online game therapeutically to get more sleep and lead a less destructive life. He would play instead of using the serotonin-inducing medications his doctor prescribed.

## WHY HAVE ONLINE GAMES COME TO OCCUPY SUCH A PROMINENT PLACE IN POPULAR CULTURE?

Bonnie Nardi (2010, p. 123) expands upon Seay and Kraut's (2007) framework of "problematic use" to include social aspects of gaming in the broader arguments concerning the term addiction and its constructs. Especially helpful is how she highlights addiction as a "cultural term in the game community as well as a clinical term used by psychiatrists and psychologists" (2010, p. 125). In this book, I draw attention to the discursive tensions one finds in arguments regarding addiction to online games in the various instances described henceforth.

The motivation behind this journey was fueled by an urge to make sense of and question the controversies surrounding "online game addiction." Having been a gamer since the early eighties, I have experienced first-hand the various contours and manifestations of online and offline digital games. I was wholly unsatisfied with the ways of understanding and portraying games and gamers that I came across in mass media and academic discussions. It seemed fitting that I marry my training in sociocultural anthropology and communication scholarship to contribute an investigation into the culture surrounding online games. This work is designed to contribute a more nuanced and grassroots (from the ground up) perspective to the debates surrounding digital gaming and its place in society.

Online gaming has been recognized as a vehicle that enables, rather than hinders, social interaction and it has been especially encouraging to see notable in-depth and qualitative inquiries in the field of game studies (Dovey & Kennedy, 2006; Meyrowitz, 1985; Nardi, 2010; Pearce, Boellstorff, & Nardi, 2009; Taylor, 2006). I feel fortunate to have had intellectual connection with those conducting these studies of gamers as they helped foster the growth of a relatively new field of intellectual inquiry, legitimized by increased opportunities for teaching and research impact in these areas. In my own pursuit of this research as well as in everyday conversation, I have been frustrated by a disproportionate number of stereotypes and cliché memes such as the "helpless addicted gamer," Asians as techno-fetishists, gamers as obese loners in their mother's basements, and the like, upon which mainstream media has profited for years.

Even more troubling is how these memes have been dominating the mainstream discussion and serving to sway public opinion and policymakers toward more negative attitudes about gaming and what it means to be a gamer. Being interested in how society shapes technology and vice versa, I wanted to examine how people's lifestyles are in dialogue with gaming in international contexts. Feeling a sense of responsibility to a community of which I have always felt a part, it was important to point to a varied set of motivations people may have to engage in this activity, as there would be with any other hobby. Showing how gaming is a normal activity people use to communicate with one another in their community was what initially compelled me to head to Korea to first conduct research on this topic almost ten years ago.[1] Therefore, this work serves as an examination of society and technology in the context of a gaming culture. Those interested in technology, policy, and innovation as they are affected by culture, social structure, and infrastructure will perhaps find the content helpful in their own work.

## PURPOSE OF THE STUDY

This work was born out of a desire to have a conversation with scholarship that was pushing back against dominant paradigms of addiction. This included the psychological and biomedical models of understanding online game addiction, and my work that built upon the critical perspectives of Bruce Alexander (2008), Stanton Peele (1989), and Jeffrey Schaler (2000), to bring ethnographic, culturally informed modes of critique to the discipline(s) of Game Studies and Communication, with which my own scholarship was evolving.

As the title of the book suggests, I argue that games and play is really a social, as opposed to an antisocial, form of responding to one's everyday life and context. After two decades of concerted research, I maintain that society should regard online gaming as a medium of communication and mode of sociotechnical transformation, rather than reduce it down to a deceptively simple term like, "addiction," which implies a need to regulate and, worse, medicate. Thus, the mission of this study has been to make a case for a nuanced understanding of the place of online games in everyday life by looking at the intersection of technology and culture.

Primarily, the three main questions driving my inquiry have been:

1. What factors have contributed to the prominence of online gaming culture in contemporary Korea?

2. How have online games played a role as a communication medium?
3. How has the figure of gaming interacted with the ground of a local context such as Korea's?

On the ground in Korea, the pervasiveness of online gaming is evident when flipping television channels and seeing professional online game tournaments akin to the spectacle of North American professional sports, along with the ubiquitous PC bang[2] signs that dot the skyline of urban Seoul. Examining emergent practices in Korean society has been vastly interesting to me, as it is a culture that has internalized online gaming as part of everyday life. Kline, Dyer-Witheford, and de Peuter note that the Korean game industry has become a key node in the "networked environment of virtual capitalism," through its rapid growth of users, along with the structure and dynamics of the interactive game business (2003, p. 169). I have been fascinated by the factors for how and why gaming has become so popular in this national context, in contrast to other countries like Canada and the United States, where games and gamers are but a mere subset of "geeky activities" and have not been in the mainstream public consciousness as it is in Korea. This ethnographic look into the nuances and complexities of this dynamic nation serves as a look at how people create meaning with their technologies and everyday circumstances. In his search for cultural meaning, Clifford Geertz follows Weber in that, "man is an animal suspended in webs of significance he himself has spun" (1973, p. 5).

Accordingly, my inquiry involved a search for just such webs of significance in Korean culture with reference to the social role played by online games as explored by Simon (2007) in how they mediate communication between nodes of meaning.

The following chapters explore how games may be viewed as a medium of cultural communication, which has been a primary research concern of mine for the better part of two decades. In this study, I aim to provide a comprehensive examination of what is, and has been, taking place in the Korean technocultural landscape in order to act as a counterweight to the dominant media discourses of helpless gamers, (Asian) technology addicts/ Techno-Orientalism, deviance, and numerous other oversimplifications.[3] This pervasive sensationalism exists in direct tension with those of everyday gamer communities, whose everyday lived situations tell a very different story. Put another way, "to seek for evidence of the 'effects of media violence' is to persist in asking simplistic questions about complicated social issues" (Buckingham, 1997, p. 67).

Wishing to personally engage with the stories of actual people involved, I sought to work toward more research that did not use addiction as a prefabricated construct. It was important to ensure that as policymakers were increasingly brought into situations that regulated the lives and habits of gamers, that they were empowered with more perspectives that did not immediately equate online game spaces with harm and pathological use.[4] Most importantly, I wanted to show the less common story of gamers benefiting socially from the game communities of which they were a part. In my attempt to show that meaning can be derived from the supposedly cold, scientific world of information and communication technologies, my research conveys the insights of gamers themselves, regarding their own understandings of their activities.

## GAMES AS COMMUNICATION

In *Understanding Media,* Marshall McLuhan declared, "In the electric age we wear all mankind as our skin" (1994, p. 47). Being heavily influenced by McLuhan through my training in Canadian Communication thought, I used this theoretical orientation to frame my own investigation into the cultural contexts and resultant debates of the current moment. As a starting point, I situated my ethnographic work in the broader game studies literature as a sociocultural study of gamers in context from a communication perspective. I was drawn to an understanding of media in McLuhan's terms: as an extension of the self (Babe, 2000; McLuhan, 1994; McLuhan, Staines, & McLuhan, 2003; Onufrijchuk, 1993). After seeing for myself how much more form mattered than content in the field, I found that the dialectic between technology and human will that McLuhan established in his work was a useful way to approach my research for this work.

The debate surrounding the positive and negative effects associated with media use long precedes online gaming. For example, one may find evidence of media panics dating back thousands of years, such as the sin of reading silently in the fourth century time of St. Augustine. Additionally, much harm has been done since McLuhan's time in the promotion of a specific brand of media research that either focused too much on the specifics of the content or its dystopian effects with little or no regard for the role played by the user except as a helplessly passive consumer of media. Evidence of this viewpoint can be found especially in the body of scholarship focused upon the television era, which includes Neil Postman's *Amusing Ourselves to Death* (1985) and Joshua Meyrowitz's *No Sense of Place* (1985). Moving into the Internet era, media seems to experience a further divorcing from oneself, as exemplified by Sherry Turkle's *Life on the Screen* (1995), which discusses the user's identity as fragmented and multitudinous as a mere result of being online and able to role play, and more recently the appropriately titled, *Alone Together* (2011), which has gotten much attention as its assertions contradict the increasingly public and social nature of media. Rather than perpetuate the notion of anomie in Western literature, Korean youth occupying the crossroads of sociality—including the social behavior I observed in and around PC bangs—are not "Bowling Alone" (Putnam, 2000) in the sense that online worlds somehow usurp offline realities. Though these contributions increase public dialogue to the benefit of media communication research as a whole, I wish to foreground the user in my own work here.

McLuhan's theories seemed to be the best way for me to structure what I had been experiencing in my research, as he regarded technology as an extension of the self instead of something that exists in opposition. McLuhan's ideas have gotten more attention since the 1994 MIT Press edition of *Understanding Media* (with an introduction by Lewis Lapham), published thirty years after the original. In 1996, *Wired* magazine captured the popular imagination of the digital revolution in its article (Wolf, 1996) concerning McLuhan's thinking, calling him its "patron saint." In *Media and the American Mind: From Morse to McLuhan*, Daniel Czitrom (1982) declared that the most fertile approach to media studies is through an understanding of Canadian Communication theorists McLuhan and his mentor Harold Innis.

Something I found especially helpful as I prepared for my doctoral fieldwork was McLuhan's concept of figure and ground as found in *Laws of Media* (1988), which was the guiding principle behind his famous statement "The medium is the message." He used the figure/ground dichotomy to look at communication technology (figure) and explain its function in a particular context (ground). He believed that in order to adequately assess the impact of a new technology, one had to examine the figure and ground (medium and context) together. To look at one or the other independently, divorced of its historical context, was more or less pointless.[5] Angus (2000, pp. 104–112) argues that prominent media scholar Raymond Williams (1974) mostly misinterpreted McLuhan's theories. For Williams, the message is key, as opposed to the medium. However, following Angus, I find McLuhan's view that the medium is the message more productive for what I am attempting to communicate. After having done multiple fieldwork sojourns, I am more convinced than ever that the games function as a communication medium (form) and the understanding of their role extends far beyond the message (content) to explain why most Koreans choose to play online games. The medium determines how people interact with content.

McLuhan saw the splitting and dividing of figure and ground as an obfuscation of true and accurate technological assessment and a means of control. "In fact, it is the technique of insight, and as such is necessary for media study, since no medium has its meaning or existence alone, but only in constant interplay with other media" (McLuhan, 1994, p. 26). McLuhan cites three reasons why the medium is the message:

1. The present environment, itself made up of the effects of previous technologies, gives rise to new technologies.
2. These technologies each, in turn, further affect society and individuals.
3. All technologies have assumptions about time and space embedded within their design and use.

McLuhan believed that an examination of figures and grounds would allow people to critically assess technology's role in society. The analysis of both a technology and its context would lend true understanding, that is, the meaning found in the message being conveyed by the medium. McLuhan's (1994, p. 10) use of an anonymous stanza is particularly fitting to describe the discussion at hand:

> In modern thought, (if not in fact) Nothing is that doesn't act,
> So that is reckoned wisdom which Describes the scratch but not the itch.

The above stanza is appropriately used in this case to represent a gap in media scholarship looking at figure (scratch) and ground (itch). For the purposes of this work, McLuhan's perspective acts as a counterweight to the many lopsided studies that simplistically interpret a high amount of media use as a pathological condition. Furthermore, I am extending McLuhan's analysis of media to delve deeper into the sociocultural relationships with technology with my inclusion of ethnographic fieldwork of user environments—to look at the place between the scratch and the itch.

The media theories of Marshall McLuhan continue to have salience in the understanding of contemporary technologies of media, arguably to a greater extent in this present Internet age than at the time of their conception in the mid twentieth century. Not only do his theories have new relevance for the current forms of media we have at our disposal, but I argue that the combination of available media and cultural variation in their use, as exemplified in Korea, brings his theories to a new level of relevance for the field of communication. By examining the contextual and subjective meaning in using a communication medium such as online games, I will illustrate the importance of evaluating both a technology and the role it plays in the sociocultural milieu in which it is deployed, in order to truly understand the nature of the phenomenon.

## FOCUS ON KOREA

In this work, my focus is the Republic of Korea (South Korea) and its online game culture, which has been simultaneously lauded and derided in local and international media. The swift growth of online gaming in Korea has served to point out the economic miracle that modern Korean society represents (Kim, 2011)—commercial and consumerist lifestyles where sophisticated and futuristic hardware is commonplace. In the years since the Korean War (1950–1953), the southern half of the world's last divided country has managed to transform from a feudal agrarian society into a flagship knowledge/information society.

This research seeks out a sociocultural explanation for the oft-celebrated success of South Korea's gaming industry and correspondingly frenetic mainstream online gaming culture. From a North American point of view, governmental, medical, and legal communities have used events in South Korea to inspire, defend, or initiate decisions regarding how they want games or gamers to be treated (Clark & Scott, 2009) (in every sense—clinically or otherwise). The tendency toward biomedical discourses (and treatments) being cut and pasted into the diagnosis of online gaming as a problem has been troubling, as has its ability to garner widespread blame as the root of social pathology in the public imagination. Journalistic linkages between the tragic high-school shootings in Columbine (1999), or at the postsecondary level at Virginia Tech (2007) and the perpetrators' video game activities are a key example of the sensationalist coverage informing the public about the entirety of games and gamers as a seriously troubled population. Even more troubling is that these discussions typically influence attitudes, which then become public policy, serving to (in most cases wrongfully) sanction the activities of an inert majority. Now living in the US with a young child, the Sandy Hook (2012) and Uvalde (2022) shootings continue to play out in the media in much the same way. As the COVID-19 pandemic rages on, I am bereft, and in many ways resolute in carrying forth with this work.

## CHAPTER OVERVIEW

This chapter presents my rationale for approaching South Korea as a fieldsite, the ethnographic methodology employed, and with the events as they occurred in the conducting of this study as a whole. First, I explain my rationale for using an anthropological approach in my ethnographic examination of a communication phenomenon. Micronarratives were an important aspect of my work, and hence why my training in anthropology and the ethnographic mindset played a large role in the design of this research. Second, there is a brief summary of event milestones, which act as background knowledge for my research stay as well as describing various opportunities to have greater participation in the inquiry into Korea's dynamic technological society. I will describe the fieldwork designed in accordance with my ethnographic field plan and the outcomes, which continue to present themselves. Third, I reveal some preliminary thoughts and reflections on my work here thus far. Finally, the rationale for methodological and field choices made will become clear as I transition from the foundations laid out in this chapter to the research findings undertaken in the later chapters.

## COMMUNICATION TECHNOLOGIES, ANTHROPOLOGICAL APPROACHES

This work synthesizes anthropological methods to investigate the meaning-making practices using communication technologies. In McLuhan's discussion of retribalization, he notes a marked difference in speed of actions in the mechanical age with the actions in the present (at the time) electric age. "Slow movement insured that the reactions were delayed for considerable periods of time. Today the action and the reaction occur almost at the same time. We actually live mythically and integrally, as it were, but we continue to think in the old, fragmented space and time patterns of the pre-electric age" (McLuhan, 1994, p. 4). With the instantaneous speed at which those with access to high-speed networks can conduct their everyday lives, we are seeing a simultaneous "warming" of hot media (typically low in audience participation due to high resolution and definition) and cool media (high level of participation where audience needs to fill in gaps), which has implications for how we examine media studies, and with which methodological paradigms.

The emergence of Information and Communication Technologies (ICTs) has retrieved the wonder and mysticism formerly or typically associated with magic. Such retrieval of what Katz (2006) describes as "Magic in the Air," with regards to technology, is what McLuhan might refer to as a form of retribalization and a return to traditional orality and "tribal" social structures of antiquity. However, as the late Bruno Latour (1993) argues, we have never truly achieved "modernity" in its ideal construct, but rather quite easily retreat to a more natural frame of being. One might even go so far as to argue that the isolating advances of literacy are only now being remedied in the advancement of a greater convergence of media that embraces oral/literate, participatory culture (Jenkins, 2006).

With the increasingly diasporic conditions of our present day mobile and global labor forces, the use of ICTs to anticipate and mediate interpersonal relations associated with one's sense of home (Miller & Slater, 2000) has become a facet of everyday life. With anthropology's time-honored preoccupation with diaspora, there is a natural fitting with an examination of the retribalization (McLuhan, 1994) that is occurring within imagined communities (Anderson, 1991; Feenberg & Bakardjieva, 2004; Bakardjieva, 2005) and the meanings inherent in those constructs. In addition, as lifestyle choices fluctuate through social transformation, leisure and what people believe to be leisure, recreation, and play (Sutton-Smith, 1997), our experiences have become more technologized and the records of that use (whether in data or otherwise) have taken over as representative—correctly or otherwise. My concern is what happens in the in-betweens, gray zones, and silences.

The situatedness demanded by ethnographic methods requires the examination of ICTs within embedded, and perhaps mundane, social structures and relations. Documentation of these relations may present unanticipated insights that speak to the inextricability of technology and culture. In the following section, I shall explore some technocultural insights to further illustrate ethnographic contributions to media studies.

The situatedness demanded by ethnographic methods requires the examination of online games as part of a broader system of ICTs within embedded, and perhaps mundane social structures and relations. The documentation of these relations may present unanticipated insights that speak to how technology and culture are co-constituted. The anthropological concern with the trappings of cultural symbol, myth, and meaning provides a re-orientation of technocultural studies. The richness of the data collected through my choices of this approach will also be a topic of discussion, as are the implications for how I conducted an anthropological inquiry within a disciplinary sensibility deriving from the communication field. This chapter should give the reader an idea of the research I undertook in order to arrive at some of the results I discuss in this book.

## REFLECTIONS ON FIELDWORK

My ethnographic fieldwork on the subject of Korean online game culture spans sustained periods of on-site engagement from 2004–2016. In between the online and offline, lifecourse and significant career moves, the "data" that I draw upon to discuss this work is longitudinal with simultaneous co-affect with those who have shared my similar age(s) and stage(s)—with all the inevitable awkward in-between.

This book is a combination of theory and praxis by drawing upon insights from international ethnographic research that I have carried out in and around online gaming communities, online and offline. I was surprised at the extent to which some of my most basic questions, which made complete sense in North American contexts, did not apply very much to the Korean context. Throughout my fieldwork, there was the nagging feeling that none of "this" was what I bargained for. Yet, in a strange perverse way, it was exactly what I signed up for. It would be precisely the things I did not anticipate emerging from this type of rich data gathering that would be the most important and provide the most insight. Indeed, I found my informants, and they found me as well. The said and unsaid, along with the eating, sleeping, and breathing aspects involved in the ideals of ethnographic fieldwork make themselves apparent throughout this work.

Starting in 2003, in order to understand what would be more of my surroundings in Korea, I did one year of immersive training in the Korean language and culture prior to my first 2004 fieldwork sojourn. During that four month stay in-residence, I was welcomed into the home of a Korean family who immediately incorporated me into the everyday workings of their household. I was also affiliated as a visiting researcher at Sejong University's Institute for Technological Innovation in the Department of Business. These relationships allowed me to get an initial orientation to my sociocultural and linguistic surroundings.

I owe many of the cultural insights written from this time period to my conversations and experiences with the members of a Korean English club, whose primary objective was acquiring fluency in English through online and offline social exchange. The local membership primarily included Koreans from all over greater Seoul, expats who were generally English teachers in Korea, and random foreigners like myself. The online membership consisted of people joining in from all over South Korea, chatting on the website in both Korean and English. Knowing the position of privilege that I could potentially occupy in this club as explored in depth by Robert Prey's investigation of English acquisition in South Korea (2005), I made a deliberate effort to ensure that my presence worked within the existing parameters of the club. Through the encouragement of the executive members, I became a local member and contributed dues that went toward the rent needed for the meeting space, as well as participated in the casual discussions during drop-in club meetings. The results from that stay included ethnographic field notes, focus groups, and in-depth interviews of gamers that highlighted online gaming in Korea as a product of culture, social structure, and infrastructure (Chee, 2006, p. 228). That stay was a transformative experience, especially for how I regarded how and where gaming takes place. It served to lay the foundation on which I built another layer of research inquiry. Most importantly, getting more insight into why people game in Korea was the optimal outcome of this research.

My subsequent (2008–2009) stay allowed me to be situated within the Korean cultural milieu for a six-month period while examining the top-down mechanisms that formed the conditions for online gaming to thrive, such as government, industry, and policy factors in a global economy. With a second ethnographic fieldwork stay, I sought to build a more robust set of insights, incorporating a "top-down" look from government and industry perspectives in addition to the observations at the "grassroots." Though rife with its own affordances and restrictions, interviewing more Koreans who were stakeholders in the technological development of the nation added an extended and nuanced perspective to my previous "bottom-up" player-oriented data from 2004. I wished to create a project within a point of tension, comparing empirical evidence with more traditional theoretical frameworks concerned with the underpinnings of society and technology, in order to more fully address the nature of online gaming culture as constantly in flux. In addition to these stays oriented around my academic programs of study, the years since have permitted me to do more onsite visits through invited engagements that continue to bolster relationships and stay updated in emergent technological practices and cultural attitudes.

In insights emerging from my earliest fieldwork in Korea, I addressed some of the cultural, social-structural, and infrastructural explanations of why Koreans had an international reputation for being particularly susceptible to online games addiction (Chee, 2006). In addition to finding a whole host of factors external to any one game, such as the use of PC bangs and other social factors, the promotion and popular play of "old" games such as StarCraft has been key in creating professional online game spectacles, known as eSports, which persist to the present. T. L. Taylor (2006, 2012) has written about the professionalization of gaming, and the instrumental manner in which "powergamers" play being intrinsically different from amateur/leisure players. Dal Yong Jin has also explained in detail about the political and economic situatedness of Korean professional gamers (Jin, 2010), which is essential to understanding Korea's online gaming mediascape. My contribution here was not to be made in examining the professional gamers for whom gaming had a clear monetary and vocational aspect to their motivations, but rather the amateur and leisure gamers whose everyday lives were more of a mystery that fuelled my ethnographic inquiry in Korea.

During the 2008–2009 stay, I was primarily funded by the Korean Government Scholarship, awarded by the National Institute for International Education (NIIED) in Korea, along with the Graduate International Scholarship from the Dean of Graduate Studies at Simon Fraser University. For this particular sojourn, I received a formal invitation from the Department of Communication at Seoul National University to commence a visiting researcher stay, beginning in September 2008. Being affiliated with Korea's top university, I was able to reach out from my extant contacts to better access individuals at other Korean academic institutions, government, and industrial firms who facilitated my research in various ways. This affiliation enriched my field research, which included more interviewing of "elites" (Gubrium & Holstein, 2002) in terms of those who are more senior in status or age markers.

Due to practical circumstances such as my relatively young age, Asian ethnicity, and professional status, sometimes my encounters would be alone, accompanied, or within group functions. I anticipated that there would also be a longitudinal aspect to the research, as people I interviewed during my previous fieldwork engagements would grow and change. Consistent with the nature of conducting business in Korea, most things rely on introductions, the nurturing of social networks, and snowball-style recruiting in the way of referrals through friendship networks. In terms of formal interview data for the top-down perspective, I structured that research around the insights of six key informants from government/industry, and eight educators regarding online games in Korea. The primary objective was to garner their perspectives surrounding what factors they saw contributing to Korea's online game culture. In addition to their subject matter expertise, their input was valuable from an ethnographic standpoint precisely because of the ways they understood their lives and technocultural subjectivities.

## OBJECTS IN THE MIRROR: BOOTH BABE OR RESEARCHER?

> *I have foreign female friends, but they are all foreign looking. When I first saw you, I thought you were Korean. How you would perceive that feeling on your skin, it was interesting that you perceived the same thing. The way you do makeup, and your hair and . . . I really thought you were Korean when I first saw you.*
>
> *—Mina*

Throughout my fieldwork, it was reasonable to expect that my own situatedness came into play on numerous occasions. As I peel back the layers to this co-constituted identity and its complexities in this book, my insider/outsider status, however superficial at times, was instrumental in blending into Korean society and yet being a foreign observer viewing phenomena through my own lenses of inquiry. As with any ethnographer, sometimes my looks (age, ethnicity, gender) increased the level of access I had, and other times were a hindrance (Bergstrom, 2009). In this respect, it was very enlightening to "compare notes" with my female informants like the one I call Mina. I was curious about whether or not she, like me, perceived a difference in the way not only women were regarded, but Asian-looking women and the corresponding expectations of performance of, and adherence to, cultural norms (Kondo, 1990). Gender dynamics were always an interesting point of discussion, and part of the motivation for writing this book has been the ability to respond to different contexts in academia, government, and industry, as I carved out more space to take on these nuances in my own published work on gender and the games industry (Chee, 2016; Chee, Hjorth, & Davies, 2021).

Early on, the realities of navigating the games industry for myself were baffling and sometimes utterly depressing, at times devolving into periods of dark cynicism. As many now know about gender-based harassment, it does not matter how one may be dressed as a reliable way to control the way people respond to oneself. One may be dismissed as a "booth babe" or a "hostess" who serves a decorative function despite providing a business card. It was not so much that I was the one at times being dismissed, as my age, gender, ethnicity, and small stature tend to make that a perennial expectation of mine. What disturbed me more was the realization of the limited role someone who looked like me might play in these professional contexts. Seeing the legions of women employed for the purpose to which I personally took exception caused me to reflect at length my own position, privilege, and performances. Not to be pessimistic too early, at various industry events I would introduce myself to the women, only to confirm that their presence as attractive women was the only thing required of them, and that they were otherwise in no way involved with games or gamers. Moreover, without a "foreign woman" sign above my head and simultaneously exhibiting Korean fashion/aesthetics, they would look at me in even greater confusion, wondering how it came to be that I was actually a games researcher and not even woefully on my way to permanent spinsterhood as was the stereotype of female graduate students, especially in a PhD program. It must make even more sense now to the reader why, when I first found Mina at one of these events, I clung to her even more tightly, due to her rarity in those nascent days. During our chat, we talked about the expectations of Korean women compared with other visibly foreign women in Korea, which brought up some interesting points, which I discuss in the section of this book regarding women in the games industry. My experiences, along with the candid stories shared amidst both camaraderie and frustration, helped guide and form my research into the systemic reasons women enter, endure, and often disengage from their work in the industry.

## DATA COLLECTION AND ANALYSIS

Ethnographic data was collected in fieldnotes through participant observation, informal interviews, formal interviews, focus groups, and open-ended surveys. While in the field and upon my return to my home in Vancouver, I transcribed my audio recordings, coding and analyzing them by hand. Due to the ethnographic nature of the research and deep engagement with my site of research, I felt it necessary to avoid outsourcing my transcription or analysis work. It was perhaps an idealistic and sometimes tedious approach, but I did not use social science analysis software for my analysis. My question is always, "How do you code for silence?" which, as Geertz notes for the interpretive ability of ethnographers, is part and parcel with distinguishing between a twitch and a wink (Geertz, 1973, p. 6). Reading between the words, knowing why someone said, "Umm . . ." and awkwardly laughed, is why having been there is important. The analysis continuously took place in the preparation, conducting, transcription, analysis, and writing periods. In large-scale projects this is not always possible or desirable, but for the outcomes of my study, this was the personal methodological choice I made for this research write-up in order to further hone my interpretation of the field data. Using my findings from the field I then compared the empirical findings with the theoretical literature to produce the synthesis found in this thesis.

Pseudonyms have been used, or informants anonymized, with identifying characteristics eliminated as appropriate. Quotes are used directly when they contribute to this ethnographic narrative of Korean online gaming culture, and their origin deliberately remains opaque. I have ensured that the data maintains its original integrity and intention while taking care to not compromise my informants. Michael Zimmer's (2010) study on the ethics of research on Facebook has provided a useful cautionary tale of the current power of data, networks, and ability to deduce identities in research. In that same study, he quotes Eszter Hargittai's insights that it is not difficult to figure out identities with only a few characteristics in certain networks.

Unlike the anthropology of old, contact with one's informants does not stop with leaving the field (or, in the case of some virtual ethnographies, upon logging off). The in-person interviews and ethnographic work has, in a sense, never halted. I am able to constantly keep in touch with those I have met through various technologies as friends and also if the need arises for follow-ups. It is also the case now where one's informants keep up and read the research they helped to facilitate and inspire. The need for identity protection on my part has been especially important for informants, as cybersleuthing someone's identity online is enabled, and the community is so relatively small at times. The pledge of "do no harm" was maintained to the best of my ability, which meant lots of discussions off the record. Those discussions were enlightening, but not explicit in these pages. Indeed, it has been fascinating and this research—as much as it is a moment in time—continues to evolve.

## AN ETHNOGRAPHIC APPROACH

The methodology most identified with anthropological research is ethnography (Agar, 1996; Clifford, Marcus, & School of American Research, 1986; Geertz, 2000; Marcus, 1998; D. Miller & Slater, 2000), which grew out of the descriptive and interpretive writing of culture in a time when the British Empire was attempting to understand the new people with whom it came into contact. Through the ethnographic method, with which many media scholars are now familiar (Allen, 1994), interested parties were able to understand the various cultural differences in the most basic workings of everyday life in order to function and communicate between various tribes. In essence, the ethnographer is the medium who, like communication theorist Marshall McLuhan, is seeing a resurgence of relevance due to increasingly uncharted cultural territory as the globe becomes more like a village.

## NEW MEDIA ETHNOGRAPHY

Contrary to perspectives common in the first generation of Internet scholarship in the social sciences, as exemplified by Turkle (Turkle, 1995; 2011), scholars such as Daniel Miller and Don Slater (2000) and Wellman and Gulia (Wellman & Gulia, 1999) have subsequently argued that the Internet is not a monolithic or placeless "cyberspace," but instead is a system composed of numerous separate technologies used by a wide variety of people in diverse geographical locations and social sensibilities.

The emergence of broadband and other ICTs has accelerated the appearance of a type of participatory culture worldwide (Jenkins, 2006). This development was also predicted by prominent scholars concerned with the changing dynamics of technology and society (Feenberg, 1999; Negroponte, 1995; Rheingold, 2002). In this light, these developments in new media draw attention to the potential gains of using an ethnographic approach in order to see how Internet technologies in particular are being used in various contexts. In the ideal outcome of an anthropological approach, the question goes beyond the "use" or "effects" of a new medium to include insights into the culture. In essence, the combination of methods I am choosing to employ for this study fits McLuhan's assertion that the medium is the message, along with his call to investigate figure (medium) and ground (context) simultaneously, rigorously, and systematically (1988).

The Internet appeared at precisely the right moment to substantiate postmodern assertions regarding the increasing abstraction and lack of depth in contemporary mediated reality because of their perspectives on identity. The viewpoints of scholars in the early 1990s pointed to a new space in which identity could be detached and thought of as something different from embodiment, exemplified by Donna Haraway's ground-breaking "A Cyborg Manifesto" (1991), Sherry Turkle's *Life on the Screen* (1995), and scholarship heralding the rich and critical scholarship of the aughts such as Lisa Nakamura's *Cybertypes* (2002).

I found the corresponding resurfacing of McLuhan's theoretical relevance regarding media as extensions of the self, have important contributions to make in terms of what they say about current technocultural practices.

For example, in thinking through affinity groups in communities online, McLuhan's discussion of retribalization was important to note as, "tribal cultures cannot entertain the possibility of the individual or of the separate citizen. Their ideas of spaces and times are neither continuous nor uniform, but compassional and compressional in their intensity" (McLuhan, 1994, p. 84). In McLuhan's rumination is the re-emergence of a necessity to assess kinship and interdependence as cornerstones of communication. Some social phenomena simply require someone to draw attention to what everyday actors in a situation have, in McLuhan's terms, become too numb to see for themselves or even think their actions to be considered culturally significant at all. He refers to Werner Heisenberg, in *The Physicist's Conception of Nature*, who points out that "technical change alters not only habits of life, but patterns of thought and valuation" (McLuhan, 1994, p. 63). The anthropological concern with the trappings of cultural symbol, myth, and meaning provides a re-orientation of technocultural studies (Bell, 2006; Dourish & Bell, 2011). Dourish and Bell (2011) have discussed "methodology" formally, "to encompass not just the craft methods and techniques that a discipline employs to do its work . . . but also the epistemological foundations of the discipline, and the ways in which methods feature as part of a broader set of conversations" reconnecting theory with practice (2011, p. 62).

The long, protracted stays in the field that are emblematic of classic anthropological works, combined with thick ethnographic description (Evans-Pritchard, 1971/1940; Geertz, 1973; Malinowski, 1964) and opacity, have led many to question the utility and "actionable insights" arising from such research. However, examples of ethnographic inquiries with profound insight have only been growing in prominence. Indeed, the ethnographer as both "medium" and "messenger" is very apparent in just a few instances described here.

Reading about anthropologists like Bonnie Nardi (2010), who studied users of technology, served as inspiration for me to delve deeper into that area of study. Julian Orr's (1996) study at Xerox revolutionized technological maintenance, customer care, and design by highlighting the particularities of relationships of service technicians not readily apparent to those with high-level decision-making powers. In a direct application to the study of media, an anthropologist conducting research for Intel (Bell, 2006, p. 141) drew attention to the uproar that ensued when Finnish mobile phone users were no longer permitted to receive text messages from a person whom they believed to be Jesus Christ. This study was particularly effective in illustrating that technology, meaning, and spirituality could and would be linked—something that was not immediately obvious in strictly technological accounts of users. Lending anthropological insight about technology, Bell critiques the impetus behind the development of "always-on connectivity and constant updating," (2006, p. 151) and their potential discord with various forms of religious practice and expression. The design, policy, and business implications arising from such studies are drawing an increasing amount of attention by those involved in the manufacture of products and services, who would benefit from an understanding of cultural practices and meaning making. The convergence of meaning and technology as it becomes more ubiquitous is therefore a positive trend and exemplified in humanistic studies of technology (Dourish & Bell, 2011; Greenfield, 2006), though still far too few.

In the tradition of material culture analysis, anthropologists are as much concerned with how subjects are constituted within material worlds as with how they understand and employ objects (Nardi, 2010; Nardi & Miller, 1990). Furthermore, attempts at hybridized approaches with political economy (Jin, 2010) that utilize macroeconomics and meaning-making practices within communities are currently in a state of tension in their examinations of macro factors within micro contexts, but represent a sense of optimism in this mode of inquiry.

However, due to one of the entry points of this work being "moral panics in the media" as it pertains to addiction, I was primarily drawn to the concept of the individualization of public problems (Gusfield, 1996) (such as alcohol and online gaming addiction). This called for a multifaceted approach that I found needed a political economic approach to analysis. While "purists" might not wish these macro and micro perspectives to blend, I have found an open and interdisciplinary approach has allowed me to carry out the work in this area to an extent that makes use of my methodological sensibilities and disciplinary training in communication anthropology and sociology. In international contexts that could utilize more insight into how technologies designed "elsewhere" are used, I wish to be one of a growing number of researchers drawing attention to how much cultural insights are needed in the very sectors, such as technology, where they have been pushed aside in favor of the "hard and fast" data.

By engaging in this first-hand, multimethod, ethnographic study, I attempt to provide cultural context and some possible explanations for why gaming and its associated activities seem so immersive and compelling in Korea. Numerous reports produced by firms such as PricewaterhouseCoopers (PwC) already detail the success of the global powerhouse that is Korea's multibillion dollar online gaming industry (Jin, 2010; PricewaterhouseCoopers, 2006, 2007, 2008), but what are the stories and accounts behind those numbers? Going beyond investigating the content of specific games, my study was driven by the desire to report on an in-depth look at culture, social structure, and infrastructure that might cast the nation's reputation for excessive online gaming in a different light. In addition to that, there has been more work in the last decade as to how professional games, spectatorship (Taylor, 2018), and the broader eSports industry has evolved worldwide. My work examines the current situation as an outcome of decades of cultivation (deliberate and otherwise) in game culture.

The fieldwork and lived experiences, engagements, that underpin my arguments in this book serve to add perspective to game research by highlighting sociability as it is created in the interactions between players, online and offline. Having outlined the rationale for choosing an ethnographic approach to examining online gaming as it is situated in a cultural context, the following section explains the particular site of inquiry: South Korea.

## WHY KOREA AS A FIELD SITE

My interest and subsequent ethnographic study of Korea began as a response to my frustration with how games and gamers were being portrayed in mainstream media as mindless drones, helpless children, or social outcasts, who were enslaved by the powers of digital games. This mode of entertainment, should we (the public) allow it to continue, would, according to the critics, herald the end of productive civilization as we knew it. Moral panics over media use are nothing new (Debord, 1983). This is ample evidence of other forms of media over the centuries that caused concern and have been folded into the normalized media ecologies of the cultures in which they reside. At present, however, public concern surrounds online gaming in large part because of the constantly shifting perception of the role it plays in the lives of youth. A key flashpoint for this concern is Korea.

Reactions to "games" as a category writ large are mixed in how they are framed ideologically (Bogost, 2007), but as one may expect, with a greater bias toward negative aspects. On the one hand, there are the celebratory or instrumentalist accounts of how games are good for cognitive development and maintenance (Chen, 2009; de Freitas & Griffiths, 2008), problem-solving (McGonigal, 2011), questioning its role in the digital economy (Dyer-Witheford & de Peuter, 2009; Jin, 2010; Kline et al., 2003), individual social mobility (Taylor, 2012), and health (Wilkinson, Ang, & Goh, 2008). On the other hand, the same games can be criticized for eliciting addictive behaviors (Alexander, 2008; Griffiths, Davies, & Chappell, 2003; Young & de Abreu, 2011), diminishing grades at school, or inciting violence (Desai, Krishnan-Sarin, Cavallo, & Potenza, 2010). In my research of game communities, I have found a number of rather panicked articles describing the pathological level at which Korean youth in particular were playing games, the strongest examples of which are Gluck (2002), Ho (2005), J. H. Kim, Lee, Kim, and Kim (2006), and T. Kim (2005), as noted in Chee (2006, p. 226). These perspectives pointed to a broader journalistic trend that indicated gamers were both troubled, and in trouble.

Having interviewed people who had told me about their complex reasons for online gaming in other ethnographic studies (Chee & Smith, 2005; Chee, Vieta, & Smith, 2005), I was still dissatisfied with the research that took for granted the diagnosis of games addiction in psychological terms. Such studies seemed to address a limited number of variables and controls without considering the sociocultural nuances of player motivations (van Schie and Wiegman, 1997; Whang, 2003). I wanted to address the phenomenological aspects of gaming in Korea at the grassroots level. That is, I wanted to investigate the reasons why everyday people in Korea played online games. Phrased as a question, what was underneath the surface of panic in mass media regarding youth supposedly on a runaway train toward a dismal future in a nation of online game addicts? After all, according to Ursula Franklin in *The Real World of Technology*, technologies are developed and used within a particular social, economic, and political context (Franklin, 1999, p. 51). I wished to use ethnography in order to look at the micro circumstances as they interacted with the macro forces (Padgett, 2003). The meta-message I wanted to convey through my analysis was that Korea is not the "mysterious other," to be exoticized and feared amidst what others have charged with Techno-Orientalist discourse (Hjorth, 2006, 2011). With so many sociocultural and historical factors to consider, an analysis without those contextual elements would be at a deficit. I wanted my ethnographic text to represent another truth other than the "Truth" circulating in greater numbers in the popular and academic communities already.

The academic research concerned with games, hailing from social and natural sciences alike, seemed to echo the (moral) panic that news agencies were all too eager to celebrate at that point. Dangerous precedents were being set with cases like Sean Wooley (Chee & Smith, 2005), whose mother was suing Sony Online Entertainment because she attributed her son's suicide to his EverQuest play. The tendency to assign blame to games and gamers was troubling to me, and I felt that I needed to be a part of ameliorating this state of affairs. There had to be a counterweight to these arguments.

In my work, I have probed the question of what constitutes disorders and if gameplay can be explained as simply an "addiction to games." Because the literature on online gaming tended to proceed with research on addiction as a foregone conclusion, I decided to problematize the term itself and urge people to re-evaluate the phenomenon of online gaming in popular culture. While the question of addiction has touched numerous activities such as heroin, alcohol, sex, ad nauseum, my inquiry focuses on games as a medium around which people also gather, congregate, and socialize. I would be reluctant at this point to make claims about these other aspects when other research focuses exclusively on such matters more thoroughly than I am able to here, and the debate rages on (Alexander, 2008; Peele, 1989; Rapping, 2000; Schaler, 2000). These inquiries, along with my own, sought to lend personal perspectives of those who spend time in virtual worlds and online games of many genres. It became clear that this debate would not go away anytime soon, but rather manifest in a slightly altered form the next time another form of emergent media became popular enough to warrant public attention.

In the way of biographical information, having started playing video games before even starting formal schooling, I knew from my own experience that gaming could be a very social experience. Further, there were also many different types of games out there, but everything was being painted (or rather tarred) with the same brush. A perennial debate is whether or not gamers should be treated psychologically or even physiologically (Clark & Scott, 2009; Young & de Abreu, 2011). My search for nuanced understandings of the motivations of gamers brought me to the works of an ever-growing cadre of scholars who are cornerstones of the global conversation on the social conditions of games and gamers (Boellstorff, 2008; Castronova, 2005; Consalvo, 2007; de Castell & Jenson, 2007; Dibbell, 1998; Dovey & Kennedy, 2006; Itō, 2009; Malaby, 2006; Nakamura, 2008; Nardi, 2010; Taylor, 2006). I hope that my work adds to this conversation in how it illustrates the complexities inherent in studying the role of gaming in different cultures.

After exploring the construction of addiction and pursuing the activity of online games as more of an attempt at community formation, I was increasingly sensitized to the discourses and representations of gamer culture, to which I myself belong. This archetypal representation of the hapless game addict as discussed above was compounded further by Techno-Orientalist discourses where an entire nation, ethnicity, or continent could be reified as hopeless techno-fetishists or completely dismissed altogether as "Other." This was the time when my research trajectory turned toward looking at

South Korea as an instance of how online gaming has played an instrumental role in sociotechnical transformation of a population. Explaining my work in this light shall be my task for the remainder of this book.

## NOTES

1. Unless emphasis requires otherwise, Korea here means South Korea.
2. Translates to "PC room" in Korean.
3. A particularly vivid example of such a case involves the swirl of media coverage surrounding the Virginia Tech Massacre of 2007 involving Cho Seung-hui, whose Korean ethnicity and video game playing were alleged contributions to his shooting rampage that killed 32, wounded 17, and included his suicide. It is interesting to note that while these aspects of the story were in the foreground, discussions of his access to firearms or possible mental illness were discussed in smaller numbers.
4. An example of irrational fear of online activities such as gaming includes the 2009 warning from the US Federal Trade Commission's (FTC) consumer alert: "The anonymity that avatars provide can encourage people to 'act out' behaviors that may be considered inappropriate, particularly for tweens and teens. Indeed, visitors may find the online equivalent of a red-light district, with simulated sexual activity or violence" (Federal Trade Commission Consumer Alert 38).
5. For example, some countries like the Philippines have mostly skipped over landlines altogether in favor of mobile phones, illustrating the need to evaluate a technology in terms of its context of implementation.

*Chapter 2*

# The Rise of Digital Game Culture in Korea

*Then I finished my juk for breakfast, and went back to my place to change into more appropriate walking shoes. I thought I'd be walking quite a bit because my intention was to go up north to the Myeongdong area and see what the PC bang/café situation was like there. As I was walking along the back street toward my subway station, I came across a dusty construction site, punctuated with red and yellow "PC BANG" signs. Intrigued, I detoured from my path and trekked up the stairs ...*

*On the third floor, I was met with a World of Warcraft banner, and behind it, the entrance to a relatively nice café with faux wood benches and PCs, with the leather chairs that are now the staple of any halfway respectable PC bang.*

*Wanting to be self-sufficient, I grabbed a card at the front desk and proceeded to find my corresponding workstation, #29. I went to 29 (in the smoking section, which happened to have more going on at that point) and the Ajeossi (Korean term for "uncle") asked if I was a smoker, and I said no. So he briskly ushered me to sit at one of the workstations on the other side.*

*Frankly, I was a bit disappointed, as I didn't see (or smell) a difference because it was all the same air (and there were more gamers to observe on that side) but complied.*

*Perhaps he wanted to keep an eye on me (they don't see many females there so I am an oddity in many ways) and so I went to the other side where a couple of guys were playing casual games quietly.*

*The workstation at which I was now sitting prompted me for a Korean National ID Number (NIN) (which, as a foreigner, I did not have). I hit the other button, and the manager Ajeossi came up behind me and said because I did not have a membership at this PC bang, I had to go in through the other dialogue box and just enter the number on my card. So the Ajeossi now knew for sure I was a waegook saram (foreigner), and my having to explain my life story to him would be sure to follow.*

*As I got into the system, Ajeossi meandered back to the front desk. I felt like I should just chill out here for a while to explore the different options on the* system and soak up the "atmosphere" as it were. However, I did not do much of that, given how strange I felt with Ajeossi's eyes boring through the back of my head.

I tried logging onto my North American Battle.net account to no avail. It was also telling that the Internet Explorer browser had not been updated in a while and I kept getting the prompt to update to IE 8. I softly let out an exasperated sigh . . .

With Ajeossi milling around seeming to want to talk, I thought maybe this was a good opportunity to ask him some questions. He came over and I gave him my card and we exchanged our background stories.

When we established that I was an academic researcher interested in games (as opposed to law enforcement or the like) he attempted to show me some of the games, and upon clicking the icons there were patches he needed to install (showing some time had passed since these were accessed).

He said the popular games were Aion, WoW, and Call of Duty. Looking around, I saw some fellows playing StarCraft, and also Counter-Strike. Ajeossi told me he had an Aion account and was level 25. So he showed me his character and how he could fly around the world. I asked him if I could take pictures and I snapped a couple.

When we were just casually chatting, I asked him what the usual clientele was, and then asked if it was elementary, high school and all he said was "I don't like them to come . . . it's not good." I realized he had become more guarded with that question, given the increasingly stringent attempts at regulating the game times of students in public and private spaces. Whether or not he was making that statement for my benefit was uncertain.

I asked him what was typically the busiest time, and gesturing around the relatively roomy café, he said today (Sunday during the day) was slow, but on weekday afternoons until 11pm it was busier.

It is a 24 hr PC bang, and the wee hours of the morning 11pm-7am it costs a little more. As he was recounting his story, he told me that he had been running this PC bang for ten years, meaning three years after the IMF crisis. He said it was an investment for his "retirement," because his major from one of the top universities in Korea was in Business and he used to work in finance.

After the IMF period, his was one of the jobs that were lost in the "consolidation process." He said this to me while making a folding down motion with his hands. His rationale for starting this PC bang business was mainly for his son, but he told me his son got another job somewhere else, so he's running the PC bang instead. We talked about him having learned English in business school, as well as some Chinese (Mandarin) and half a year of Japanese, which he pointedly told me he did not like very much.

A weird moment was when I casually asked if he lived in the area. He gave me a brief look of uncertainty and told me how he used to live in the south of Seoul . . . Then all these other places. Then I asked what about now? And he gave me another look, and said, somewhat more guardedly, "From 7am, I work here . . ." and trailed off.

*I replied with "Oh . . ." as if it was my sudden realization as well. It was somewhat fuzzy as to whether or not he just slept there at the PC bang or had fallen on tough times. I could not bring myself to ask him so crassly and explicitly to confirm what our eye contact had at that moment. He did not end up naming a specific neighborhood. He merely stated, "This job . . . it's very hard."*

*It turned out that I ended up briefly meeting his son, who happened to be buzzing in and out of the café with a soapy tray and rubber gloves on. Seeing my surprise, Ajeossi quickly said to me his son happened to be in town helping to make lunch. Ajeossi also added that, "My son's wife's sister lives in Canada." Again, it was a little odd.*

*During our verbal exchange that walked the line between fluid and halting, I felt as though he was not the type of person who would outright lie to me, but he probably would not volunteer information if it was potentially embarrassing. This was definitely one of those important cases of reading between the lines, acting upon non-verbal cues, and interpreting silence at crucial moments.*

*I asked if there were any women who came to this PC bang, and he answered that his wife helped him run the place when business was slower, typically in the daytime. A telling answer that women were quite the oddity here.*

*By the time the pauses and silences got longer and we were both looking at our feet, I paid for my time and said I might come back when it was busier, and took my leave. What I did know, however, was that I had just been thoroughly engulfed in a richly ethnographic moment and I needed to make sense of what just happened.*

As far as technology is concerned, South Korea has outdone most countries in the world. It is a global leader in the production of semiconductors, cars, ships, and gadgets (Hira, Morfopolous, & Chee, 2012). Korean brand names such as Samsung, LG, and Hyundai have become commonplace in millions of households with good reason. The nation has truly undergone a reinvention and reimagination of itself, from a war-torn destitute country to a trailblazer on the information highway.

At first blush, a discussion of Korea in merely economic terms as a contemporary "miracle" (Amsden, 1989) is in line with the celebration of technology being solely responsible for emancipating nations from poverty. In a classic case of what Mosco calls the "Digital Sublime" (Mosco, 2004)—in the collective vision and belief in digital lifestyles—Korea's turn toward the panacea of the information economy has indeed been remarkable in every aspect. The extreme success of online gaming very well fits into modernist narratives, but they fall short of addressing the arduous labor, geopolitical circumstances, and cultural context for why Korea is now a technological "powerhouse" in the world. After all, as Deleuze is noted for saying, "Technology is social before it is technical" (Galloway, 2004, p. 79). Korea is a particular case that must be examined within the boundaries of its national circumstances. In the first part of this chapter, I will describe the foundational aspects of Korean social history, culture, and the present new media scene in South Korea. In the second part, I will examine the political and economic policy implications in and around the global and local game industry.

As a whole, this chapter serves to document the factors that contributed to the rise of online gaming in Korea to its current state of prominence. It shows how games and platforms in and of themselves are not the sole explanatory measure of success. That the popularity of online gaming in Korea can be attributed to key technological policy decisions in Korea is not commonly discussed in games literature. Also, deliberate choices in trade relations and restriction have influenced the path dependency of online gaming, which I will further describe.

In quoting the World Bank's description of Korean economic development, Robert Bedeski (1983, p. 3) aptly paints a picture of the economic miracle that appeared to take place in Korea:

> From a position uncomfortably close to the bottom of the international income scale and without the benefit of significant natural resources, Korea embarked on a course of industrial growth that became one of the outstanding success stories in international development.

Though the term "miracle" has been bandied about when it comes to describing the situation, decades later Meredith Woo-Cumings' (2001, p. 373) expressed dissatisfaction with the notion:

> The East Asian Miracle leaves unexplored the basic social and political underpinnings that propelled growth in East Asia. Even when it deals with the question of the role of the state in economic development, it approaches the question ideologically.

Korea has participated in an extraordinary moment in global communication history.

Along the way, subject to what Nancy Abelmann and others have called a "compressed modernity" (2003)—along with the more general shock of modernity (Cassegard, 2001)—the nation has propelled itself into becoming a bona fide networked information society (Castells, 2004). That is, even as many around the globe are still chasing that utopian notion, many find attaining that designation elusive. Drawing upon extant theoretical literature on Modernity (Feenberg, 1995; Kim, 2011), the reader will find a discussion of how notions of modernity came to be adopted and reworked to the geopolitical and social realities on the peninsula.

Through a sociohistorical discussion including Japanese colonization, the Cold War, Korean War, and subsequent political/economic ramifications that framed the workings of Korean life, I will show how the institutions emerging from those times of creative destruction came into their present form of influence today. These national factors are reflected in the discussions I had with my informants. These histories inform and mediate their understanding of Korean life.

After highlighting the sociohistorical underpinnings of Korean institutions, this chapter touches upon the place of an "education culture" within the hearts and minds of the nation.

Korea's disproportionately large investment in education, compared with other OECD countries, and emphasis on science, technology, engineering, and math fields, along with (to a lesser extent) military exemption policies have facilitated the nationwide growth of the now-pervasive online gaming.

As gaming grew in prominence, government and industry alike began to see it as an economic panacea for Korea. One cannot underestimate the role that large corporate entities, the chaebols (like Samsung, LG, Hyundai, etc.), play in almost all the affairs of Korea along with its sense of nationalism/nationhood. The chaebols and government science and technology initiatives shaped the landscape of Korean communications (Larson, 1995) and with it gaming—and continue to do so.

This discussion then turns in the direction of a global event: the Asian Financial Crisis of 1997 (Jin, 2011, pp. 31–49), which I argue was a catalytic moment that created a perfect storm of preexisting and resultant conditions for the online games scene in Korea to flourish. At the time, Korea had just realized the implementation of a nationwide broadband policy, thereby enabling high-speed Internet access throughout the country to its over 50 million inhabitants. As Stewart (2004) points out, there were various educational obstacles to achieving a sophisticated level of literacy in these technologies for the average person, even if the infrastructure was a positive step. The financial crisis, termed the "IMF Crisis" domestically, served to upend much of the extant wealth and power structures that had asserted themselves over the nation's affairs until that point. With international auditors throwing open the books and reforming the chaebols, there were many job losses. This new unemployment rocked the nation to its core, including throwing into question traditional roles determined by class, gender, and age. However, this new upheaval also gave rise to a flurry of new entrepreneurial activity by some business-savvy individuals. Moreover, according to Jin (2011, p. 45) the Korean government needed a high-level economic change in order to stimulate the economy post-1997 crisis. One of the major shifts in economic policy beginning in 1999 was an increased focus on domestic consumer marketing by encouraging credit card use and e-commerce. Korea's economic recovery could be attributed in large part to a strong recovery in consumption (Jin, 2011, p. 47).

This combination of events turned entrepreneurs toward many start-up activities, including running Internet cafes or, as they are termed in Korea, the PC bang. I have argued elsewhere (Chee, 2006) that the PC bang was a cornerstone of social interaction, serving as de facto community centers all over the country. They are the flashpoint of social interaction, especially for youth, in the hyper-urban capital city of Seoul, where more than 10 percent of the Korean population resides. The creation of these gaming centers, to the number and extent that they now occur, would not have happened were it not for the particular reverberations of the Asian economic crisis of 1997. The characteristics of Third Places—in the sense of between work/home—became complicated by the multipurpose nature of PCs, and increasingly nuanced with the proliferation of multiple activities, screens, devices, and vocational and recreational activities.

As a site of study, Korea drew me into its extraordinarily rich field of inquiry for many reasons: (1) rapid industrialization fueled by geopolitical tensions and nationalism, (2) class tensions associated with social and geographical mobility of Korean diaspora (Abelmann, 2003), complicated further by (3) a pervasive Confucian ideology (Confucius, 1979) which emphasizes filial piety, ancestral ties to the land, and subservience of youth. Moreover, scholars such as Bedeski (1983) have long noted that tensions of globalization and contemporary Western notions of the malleability of fate in terms of economic mobility have become more prevalent in modern Korea. Oh and Larson (2020) have also given specific attention to the situational factors shaping these affordances from a development perspective.

## THE RISE OF GAMING: CULTURE BEFORE POLICY

From my most profound experiences to everyday interactions, navigating authority and structure would be at the forefront of concern: given my status/standpoint, how should I do [x], with whom should I [x], and how should I conjugate my verbs given the context? I grew to relate to a broad sense of cynical pragmatism for how more things might get accomplished while also humoring the crushing weight of the bureaucratic powers that be. It was in this context that I encountered those interfacing the most with the typically tidy narratives of statecraft and technology policy.

In this respect, it seemed widely acknowledged off the record that "culture" comes before "policy."[1]

*S: If I were to say a short story about the Korean IT industry . . . a combination of the gaming and the PC room came before the government policy intervention. The culture came first. How it worked was that after the war, we had this word "palli palli." When [Koreans] took up the Internet, they got frustrated with the old copper lines. They went to the PC room so they could access [Internet] faster. They wanted more. [With the] introduction of gaming, they wanted more. [With the] introduction of StarCraft, they wanted more. So, there was the existing culture, but when it mixed with the PC room, gaming, everything exploded.*

In my investigation of events and policies precipitating the rise of online games in Korea, a dominant sentiment I encountered was that theory and policy produced an aesthetically pleasing skin in which to deliver a package of directives associated with the messy realities of culture and politics. The opinion of a manager at a government agency in Korea I interviewed exemplified the general narrative I would encounter in investigating the rise in Korean online games. He said that the biggest milestone in the path toward Korea's destination as an online games superpower was nationwide broadband Internet access, which enabled the widespread proliferation of PC bangs, and consequently online games. I asked him why he thought ICT in Korea has been successful, and why it is considered "the gaming hub of the world"? He attributed the success in Korea to online games and to the policies that have promoted the IT industry.

*The gaming industry of course . . . I have to be honest it at first wasn't considered much in the beginning, but as time passed on with the success of Lineage, then people started to get serious and consider gaming. But in terms of history, originally when [the agency] first started it was more for the purpose of helping the arcade industry. This is way back at the beginning, but as the online side grew, so [the online games agency] grew and the online grew. Arcade died off.*

Interviews such as this extremely generative one with a manager helped point me in many possible directions of inquiry. Between my primary data gathering methods and secondary research, there would be a dialogue. Though I had my interview protocols to guide the conversation, sometimes there was much to learn from just letting the subject talk about what they found most important. Pulling out themes from the topics brought up in these conversations or going on what might have perplexed me in my field notes, I would then need to delve deeper into sociohistorical materials to add focus to the picture developing in front of me. The themes in this chapter reflect the dialogue between what my informants highlighted as important to the rise of gaming in Korea, along with how history, economics, and geopolitics are important to evaluate how online games came to be in Korea as well.

## COMPRESSED MODERNITY AND GEOPOLITICS

When faced with things that surprise me in the field or otherwise, there is the desire to immediately make sense of it in its sociocultural context. So right from the beginning of my research on Korea, I made myself as aware as I could of Korean history, geopolitics, and culture, along with Korean value systems. It was clear to me that a holistic evaluation of social history needed to be part and parcel with an evaluation of online games in Korea, when even the lack of uptake in console gaming could be traced back to Korea's animosity with Japan (the homeland of console systems like Nintendo and Sega) and resultant boycott of Japanese products until just recently (Jin & Chee, 2008).

The ambivalent relations with Japan have not ended. While I was in Korea the summer of 2008, Korea and Japan were embroiled in an argument over ownership of a small island (in the "East Sea" relative to Korea, or the "Sea of Japan") between the two countries (known as Dokdo, Korea, or Takeshima, Japan). Hour after hour on television I would see government-sponsored advertisements on the issue, which would dredge up the sting of the Japanese 1910–1945 brutal colonization of the Korean peninsula. This issue was so important that the Academy of Korean Studies conference in which I participated was originally set to take place in Fukuoka, Japan but was instead pulled back to Seoul in direct protest of the Dokdo issue.

It was also an ever-present reality that while in Korea, I was technically living in a war zone. Not ten days after Japan surrendered in 1945, the Korean peninsula was partitioned along the 38th parallel by the USSR and USA into North (The Democratic People's Republic of Korea) and South Korea (The Republic of Korea). The North became led by Communist ideology with support from USSR/China and the South by American capitalism. The North ambushed the South in 1950, which began the Korean War and only ended in a ceasefire armistice treaty in 1953. Many casualties later, the two Koreas were once again partitioned along the 38th parallel with the Demilitarized Zone (DMZ) as a mine-laden four kilometer wide border between the two nations. Through colonization, liberation, partition, and various military regimes, it may come as a surprise that only as recently as 1992 South Korea had its first civilian government in more than a quarter of a century. The capital city of Seoul, where I was living, is almost right at the 38th parallel, with many North Korean missiles pointed right at the city. There are periodic skirmishes along the border to this day, with South Korean males having compulsory military service for two years and two months after high school with very few exceptions.

According to Robert Bedeski (1983), modernization in Korea became a full-fledged political program under the military rule of Park Chung Hee, who is known in the country as the architect of Korea's aggressive Five-Year Development plans that are credited with the transformation of the country from its agrarian to industrial economy in less than thirty years starting in 1962. Guided by the government, the cooperation between private investment and public credit ensured that its mixed economy grew despite its adversity following the devastating Korean War (1950-1953) and a lack of natural resources in a 100,210 square kilometer area.[2] Despite regime changes, this aggressive development model has persisted in pushing Korea from its industrial to information economy.

## KOREAN CONFUCIANISM: A BRIEF HISTORY

Yoon (2006) has analyzed Neo-Confucianism and traditional feudal structures in order to understand the emergence of cyberkids in Korea in their mobile and online modes of sociality.

Because Confucianism pervades everyday life in Korea, and is a major force in structuring social life, I have found it beneficial to draw upon Eastern philosophy in order to discuss how it has an influence on the social shaping of online games.

Confucianism is a philosophical doctrine named after Chinese intellectual Confucius (551-479 BC). It has been credited with maintaining social order in a feudal system consisting of relatively autonomous, self-sufficient, farming communities (Hong, 2004, p. 57). Along with other influences like Buddhism, Shamanism, and later Christianity, Confucianism is a dominant ideology in Korea, the principles of which may be found in family and extended to government organization.

Korean society in its present state can be said to be the most strictly Confucian. Due to Korea's position on the peninsula between Mainland China to its west and Japan to its east, the nation has traditionally occupied a position of geopolitical defensiveness, subject to persistent cultural (and biological) exchange between all three—both consensual and resisted, at various points throughout history.

Chinese Confucianism came to Korea as a result of cultural exchange between the two nations during the bloody Three Kingdoms Period (220-280 AD). Along with Buddhism and the mélange of spiritual influences, Confucian values had a great influence on the education, moral, and political systems and collective identity of Korean people (Nahm, 1993). Korea is especially intriguing, as traditional universalism typical of Confucianism appears to have been replaced by nationalism, yet still stressing Confucian tenets of "achievement, social harmony, and education as the vital means of transforming society, [along with] deference to authority, inequality in social relations, and the extended family as the basic social unit" (Bedeski, 1983, p. 13).

As Hong (2004, p. 56) writes, Confucian doctrine emphasizes the social order of a hierarchically organized state through ethical principles and codes such as Three Fundamental Principles and the Six (later Five) Cardinal Relations. The six cardinal relations include relationships between parents and children, husbands and wives, elder brothers and younger brothers, rulers and subjects, teachers and students, and between friends. These relationships are considered the pillars of society and must be upheld in order to maintain an orderly healthy society.

Because Confucianism is not a religion, but a way of life, it has been arguably more seductive and willingly adopted by Koreans of all persuasions: typically urban intellectual classes, Shamanistic Koreans in rural areas, and even Evangelical Christians. This has occurred through a series of recessions and renaissances of Confucianism, such as the Neo-Confucianism movement during the Joseon (Chosun) Dynasty of the 1400s and even more recently a rebirth of Confucianism in the late 1990s, both of which have served to maintain a semblance of social cohesion during times of national unrest and upheaval. Though one would be well-advised to avoid the trap of regarding Confucianism as an explanatory panacea, it is worthwhile to note how the explanatory and epistemological power of Confucianism gets invoked in discussions of the scholarly and everyday alike. In the following section, I explain just some of Korean societal influences, its spirituality and family dynamics.

## ALL IN THE FAMILY

Having been raised in my own primordial stew of haphazard applications and realizations through Confucianism, Catholicism, Protestant Christianity, Buddhism, and all their complications, I found Korean articulations of family quite pluralistic—often familiar. A "family" in contemporary Korean society sits at the intersection of many ideological dichotomies: Eastern and Western, local and global, collective and individualist. Given what I knew to be tendencies to project, I gathered insights about families with the guidance of everyday expressions in language and interpretation of action through as much checking in with subjects as possible.

I have been consistently interested in everyday interpretations of big philosophical traditions such as Confucianism, and less interested in the broad theoretical arguments and academic intricacies given my own complicated relationship with this background in my family (itself a product of extractive imperialist colonialism, displacement, and apartheid). Any syntheses I made were given the guidance of scholars and everyday folks I encountered in the field. Some of those insights were relevant for framing what I was seeing in terms of familial relations and culture.

Confucius made the natural love and obligations obtained between members of the family the basis of a general morality (Confucius, 1979, p. 18). The concept of a family in Korea goes much more beyond the North American conception of one's immediate "nuclear family," but is more reflective of "clan" and "kin" and "tribe." Linguistically, one's age defines how one addresses and is addressed within the household, as well as in the street. The hierarchy of language is highly present as a correlative of age and, in Korea, gender. The familial structure extends outside the consanguineal family and into modes of address within Korean society, such as calling relative strangers "sister," "brother," or "grandmother."

As previously mentioned, the ideology of the Confucian Six Cardinal Relations, with apparent age and gender hierarchies, are pervasive in Korean language and social structure. Benedict Anderson (1991) would refer to this familial stance as an "imagined community," in that it serves to conceive of the nation in a deep, horizontal comradeship such that people would be willing to sacrifice themselves for its cause.

## RECIPROCITY

Examples that appeared evident to me as Confucian notions of reciprocity were manifested through immersion in the everyday rhythms of familial life in Korean domestic contexts. I would frequently hear, "Katta-wa . . ." as a family member left for the day. In Korean, "Katta-wa," is a very informal way of saying, "Go, and come back." A Korean family member staying typically says this to another family member who is leaving the household. This imperative to go and come back extends beyond the everyday to symbolize the reciprocity inherent in the ideology that permeates Confucian thinking.

The general Confucian attitude toward reciprocity is that our obligation toward others should be in proportion to the benefit we have received from them. Intrinsic to the structure of Confucian collectivism is the mutual dependence among the relational parties, conditional on each party's realization of culturally assigned respective roles, duties, and responsibilities. That is, loyalty and obedience from those with lower social positions must be reciprocated, but this is contingent upon the higher-position partners fulfilling their responsibilities by realizing the principle of "benevolence" in their actions (Hong, 2004, p. 57).

Through my discussions and interactions on the ground, folks expressed that in contemporary Korean society, people are now caught in a type of double-bind. On the one hand, the society is structured around the deliberate privileging of the elder and male members of the family-society. The reasoning for such privileging, however, is due to the established patriarchal forms of governance and societal roles. For instance, the oldest male at the table always pays for the meal; therefore it would make sense for the oldest male to occupy the highest socioeconomic status. On the other hand, amidst charges of "ageism," "sexism," and increasingly globalized cultural practices in Korea, the expectation that the oldest male is the best-off may not always be the case, but tradition holds that he must still pay. As a result, he may get into debt, while less is expected of his subordinates who may be better off. It is one of the many ambiguities within the current social transformation occurring in Korea in the expectations of adherence to Confucian hierarchical modes of practice. While the changing nature of age and gender roles is evident in Korea at the moment, it may not be a mystery that traditionalists argue in the interests of "societal harmony," that traditional hierarchical structures continue to dominate.

In North America, where performative individualism continues to dominate, living with one's parents has and continues to broadly signal a type of "failure to launch." For many collectivist cultures, it was more an everyday reality for children to remain socially and economically beholden to their parents well into and beyond their thirties. While this may mean something different for each family, the moral aspect is important. The "moral" of the story is still that one's elders have sacrificed of themselves for the younger generations, and for that there must be reciprocity. My own upbringing reflected and privileged the notion of multigenerational household as ideal, despite our reality being quite the opposite narrative of an isolated immigrant family with its own struggles regarding cultural touchpoints and identity.

Confucian doctrine is quite explicit in the links it makes between the benevolence one shows within their family, and one's character and performance as a member of society. In The Analects (I, 2), Confucius states, "It is rare for a man whose character is such that he is good as a son (hsiao) and obedient as a young man (t'i) to have the inclination to transgress against his superiors; it is unheard of for one who has no such inclination to start a rebellion." Love for people outside one's family is looked upon as an extension of the love for members of one's own family.

The Asian economic crisis of the late 1990s saw the South Korean government urge its citizens to contribute their gold jewelry in order to boost its foreign reserves. While this request may seem unrealistic to North Americans, many Koreans did, in fact, contribute what they could from their possessions. When I asked a Korean about this phenomenon during a fieldwork stay, she told me, "We didn't think it would make much of a difference, but people did it for the symbolism of helping our country." Indeed, these "family" ties of reciprocity continue to persist and exemplify themselves in the everyday affairs of Koreans around the globe.

## AMBIVALENCE: INTERGENERATIONAL GUILT

Throughout my experiences in situ and beyond, I became interested in understanding the social mechanisms at work, and in particular the "ties that bind" folks together. That is, the social glue that compels those in a social framework to remain committed to upholding its structure.

Just as I explored Eastern philosophy for insights regarding what I was observing around me in Korea, I also looked to Western philosophy. Through the Confucian paradigm, I was seeing a lot of what seemed to be guilt, and in my readings of Nietzsche, found what he had to say about creditor/debtor relationships had some parallels worth exploring in my work.

In Nietzsche's ruminations on the ambivalent guilt of the living and dead (1989, section 19, p. 88), I found his reference to the creditor/debtor relationship to be an interesting intersectional application of reciprocity and guilt: "The civil-law relationship between the debtor and his creditor . . . has been interpreted in an . . . exceedingly remarkable and dubious manner into a relationship in which to us modern men it seems perhaps least to belong: namely into the relationship between the present generation and its ancestors."

According to Nietzsche's discussion about the original tribal communities in primeval times (1989, section 19, p. 88), "the living generation always recognized a juridical duty toward earlier generations," and that obligation to founders of the tribe was both practical and sentimental. It is only through the sacrifices and accomplishments of the ancestors that the tribe is able to exist. It is apparent that one must pay those ancestors back with sacrifices and accomplishments. However, this debt constantly grows greater and more difficult (but no less important) to satisfy as, "these forebears never cease, in their continued existence as powerful spirits, to accord the tribe new advantages and new strength" (1989, section 19, p. 89). In this sense, one is able to easily relate the present state of Confucian filial piety and ancestor "worship" that is prevalent in Korean practice.

Nietzsche asserts that in order to reciprocate adequately, sacrifices such as feasts, music, honors, and obedience must be given. One must fear the wrath of the ancestor and his power, thoroughly conscious of the debt to him, as the tribe grows more prosperous. But he also asks, "can one ever give them enough?" In the following section, I shall provide an illustrative example of the interaction between guilt, obligation, and ritual.

## JAPANESE COLONIZATION OF KOREA AS BACKDROP

Scholars of Korean history will note that the peninsula has been historically mired in the power plays of Three Kingdoms, along with tensions associated with Japan for much longer than the period indicated here (events since Japanese colonization in the early 1900s as it pertains to industrialization and computing platforms). I have discussed this period with Koreans who have indicated this time as heralding the industrialization of the country. It is one more layer to understanding the national context, by looking at the historic relationship between Korea and Japan, along with what that relationship has meant to the structuring of government, corporate entities, and policy. Japanese colonization began in 1910 and lasted until 1945. This annexation was motivated by the need to control Korean resources and to use the peninsula as a launching pad for geostrategic reasons, including the Russo-Japanese War. There were certainly negative effects and this was a period that continues to haunt the memories and in many cases the casual everyday conversation of Koreans to the present day. On one occasion, walking around Myeongdong, a busy shopping district in the center of Seoul, I came across a demonstration asking for compensation from the Japanese for the use of Comfort Women by which Korean women were forced into sexual slavery during 1932–1945 for the Pacific War (Yoshimi & O'Brien, 2000, p. 1). Related to that was the Seodaemun Prison (now a museum), which was used to imprison, torture, and execute political dissidents during the Japanese occupation, and is also a vivid reminder of this bitter time in Korean history. Both times I visited this site to learn more about this time period, I was struck on an emotional level by the feeling of collective wounds that are very much in the process of healing from traumas suffered during these times to the present day.

Given the relative freshness of the wounds mentioned above, it makes sense that the first significant event was Japanese colonization in shaping Korean industrialization in the twentieth century. State-firm relationships in Korea can be better understood by examining the evolution of the Korean state over the course of the twentieth century (Hira et al., 2012). During the Japanese occupation, the use of the Korean language was suppressed, and education was largely limited to vocational training geared toward developing a skilled workforce. It was also meant to crush Korean nationalism. According to Seth (2002), the Korean colonial state was highly subservient and limited to the prerogatives of Imperial Japan. On the other hand, there were tangible benefits that set up the groundwork for the Korean "miracle" that followed. The first is the setting up of infrastructure, including an extensive transportation infrastructure (railways and ports). Basic educational facilities, including schools were also created. Perhaps the most important benefit, however, was the development of a managerial culture and set of skills that had a lasting impact.

## CULTURAL FACTORS IN THE PRESENT KOREAN MARKET

There are a number of cultural factors to tease out in the following pages regarding how social history and contextual circumstance provide a comprehensive picture of how online gaming rose to prominence in Korea.

Having spent a significant amount of time immersed in the Korean technocultural landscape during my fieldwork, I found a number of sentiments toward technology particularly remarkable. Commensurate with the aforementioned overlap in government and industry people and practices, Korea has a significant history of active promotion of a technologically oriented lifestyle across all sectors. The prominent promotion and celebration of conspicuous consumption, often couched in nationalistic and modernist sentiments, has successfully contributed to the inclination toward technological neophilism. Enthusiasm for the latest and fashionable technologies lends itself to promoting more of a popular gaming culture than in other countries. Korea appears to have a captive, and simultaneously demanding, use culture (Kim, 2011). For example, during my time as a visiting researcher in the Department of Communication at Seoul National University, I had the opportunity to provide input on the research of graduate students. I found some of their projects interesting, primarily because it allowed me insight into what Korean graduate students found interesting about technology, culture, and the human condition in Korea. A research question that was indicative of the prevalent attitude toward technological adoption was whether or not mobile phone usage should be viewed as a human right. It showed me how mobile communication was a "powerful and natural complement to interpersonal communication in Korea" (Oh & Larson, 2011, p. 91).

## HANGUL AND THE QWERTY KEYBOARD

The government worker I interviewed stated, "The gaming experience is one of the aspects of community. The community is the real reason for people to come and play." From a linguistic point of view, products developed for the Korean public in the Korean language also increase the level of domestic adoption in content and devices. Under King Sejong (r. 1418–1450) the Korean syllabary known as Hangul was invented, and metal movable type was used in printing as early as the beginning of that century. The Korean phonetic alphabet (unlike ideographic writing systems like Chinese, for example) has enabled the rise of ICTs in Korea. The twenty-two characters easily transfer to a QWERTY type of keyboard and expressing oneself in a limited number of characters through the small spaces afforded by text messages and chat systems is easier than in most languages in the world. For example, the "bang" in "PC bang" is spelled with three symbols in Hangul (방). So, to say one word in English would take four-character spaces whereas in Korean it takes one space. One can imagine how in a forum like Twitter that limited statements to 140 characters (now 280 characters), one could express a great number of ideas in that same number of syllables, whereas in a language like English, 280 characters still conveys less information efficiently. Indeed, even at the time of introduction, the language system was a democratizing force for a population that up until then had only used the Sino character system known in Korea as Hanja. This literacy has facilitated the transfer to easily inputting characters when using electronic devices to communicate.

## FOUNDATIONS OF COMPUTING

*The communication revolution: some people saw that this could really turn things around. Because Korea already had heavy industry, all these things . . . we needed something more and they turned to the IT side.*

—*Korean Games Industry Executive*

Oh and Larson (2011, p. 83) state that through government guidance, Korea achieved what it called, "the world's best broadband infrastructure," and that by 2001, it led the world at just over half its population using the Internet. Considering that Korea's infrastructure was decimated in the middle of the twentieth century due to its Civil War between the North and the South (1950–1953), and before then its culture and language suppressed by Imperial Japan (1910–1945), it is mind-boggling to fathom the level of mobilization required in all sectors to journey from a primarily agrarian, to industrial, to its present information-centric society within such a short time. Invoking the myth of the Digital Sublime that Mosco discusses in his 2004 book of the same name, Korea is an example of how the information highway acts as a restructuring agent (Menzies, 1996). The nation currently serves as a model for many developing and developed nations for the levels of ICT usage and resulting in a modern technological life.

The success of the online gaming industry is attributed mostly to widespread Internet access, and a host of other catalysts that included aggressive government and industry promotion of a digital utopia, which was a factor in the rapid rise of technological adoption in Korea. One of my interviews with a general manager in a Korean governmental agency promoting games is especially enlightening for this discussion of public promotion of Korea's Information Society and the necessary approval and cooperation of the public.

*The government saw the value in having the whole nation connected by the Internet. They had these catchphrases, these banners or slogans. They pitched it, and it worked. People bought into it, even the companies bought into it.*

It seemed that the Korean populace was accustomed to these types of government initiatives from the Park Chung Hee era:

*In Korean: "Choose, and Concentrate," back from the Park Chung Hee era. He had this economic system . . . Every five years, we change the focus. That's how we had heavy industry, light industry. He is the one who laid out [the plans]. Of course he is criticized for being a dictator, but he laid the foundation.*

Indeed, in looking at the way the chaebols, government, and the populace at large have moved together in a relatively unified trajectory, it would be fair to say that it is through garnering the public's willingness and complicity toward the end goal that Korea is the closest the world has seen a nation come to the realization of an Information Society.

## A PERFECT STORM: 1997

In many ways, 1997 was an especially pivotal year for Korea for creating the conditions for burgeoning growth toward an Information Society. The factors that precede this transformative time, as well as unexpected events and their sociological manifestations are absolutely central to understanding the rise of Korean online gaming in its current state.

Although Myung Oh and James Larson (2011, p. xiv) have addressed similar frustrations I have experienced with international data, definitional issues, and the governmental agency data that have become canon amongst researchers, they are nonetheless important in level-setting due to their instrumental role in policymaking. They have articulated the shortcomings of an overreliance on decontextualized statistics as a persuasion tool. I present the qualitative data I have collected here as a contribution to the overall picture and encourage the evaluation of the findings on their own merit. In attempts to create a fully functional and globally competitive information economy, the Korean government, through its comprehensive Korean

Information Infrastructure plan, implemented nationwide broadband Internet access in March 1995. Within the period of 1999 to 2002 alone, the Korean government invested a total of $11 billion into broadband Internet services (Jin, 2011, p. 45). Along with this infrastructural initiative, the "Cyber Korea 21" policy focused "financial and human resources toward the technological advancement of information and communication networks and to attract investment from the private sector" (Jin, 2011, p. 45). Due to the interplay of political and economic circumstances, along with a healthy dose of state paternalism, access grew cheaper and more accessible to the everyday public.

## KOREA'S ECONOMIC CRISIS AS CATALYST

*The policy came after that mixture [of game culture and PC bangs] was already there. The policy contained it in a way that was more productive. The policy wasn't 100 percent deliberate. It's a mixture. You need the explosion to kind of push . . . You need to get the industry in a certain direction.*

—Government-industry relations insider

According to Woo-Cumings (2001, p. 363), "The crisis of 1997–98 was a disaster waiting to happen, given the highly leveraged nature of the chaebol," and that "for the period of 1988–96, corporate indebtedness of Korean firms was greater than that of practically any other firms in the world" (2001, p. 357) and a reorientation of economic policy and practice to include other things like online entertainment was essential. In order to give the reader an idea of the extent to which the economic crisis of 1997–1998 affected the everyday life of Koreans, one must explain the place of the chaebol in Korea. She states that "Koreans refer to this period as the 'IMF crisis,' making the nature and cause of the event deliberately ambiguous . . . The crisis and the subsequent bailout also inserted international financial institutions, mainly the International Monetary Fund (IMF) and the World Bank, deeply into the reform process in Korea, greatly raising the stakes of reform. The virtue of this was that the international financial institutions could run political interference for the new regime, with every unpopular policy and outcome being blamed on the IMF—from legalizing layoffs and sky-rocketing unemployment to massive corporate bankruptcy" (2001, p. 363).

In line with Confucian hierarchies, chaebols are family-type enterprises, with the CEOs as patriarchs, often literally headed by family dynasties. According to Biggart (1998, p. 316), "Samsung founder Lee appointed two sons, two daughters, a daughter-in-law, and a father-in-law to head Samsung enterprises. Professional managers were integrated into the upper echelons over time, but family ownership and patrimonial control continued to characterize Korean businesses in the 1990s." Additionally, Bedeski (1994, p. 86) outlines that a common practice is for a senior executive to "retire" and set up quasi-independent firms that are in practice part of the executive's former company. At the time of his writing (pre-crisis and subsequent reform), LG Group had sixty-two companies, and Samsung had thirty-seven sister firms. Moreover, the Korean government has been in a parent role as well, simultaneously guaranteeing and disciplining the chaebol—the four most prominent being recognizable in North America as Samsung, Hyundai, Lucky/Goldstar (now LG) for the electronics, ships, and cars that play a role in the global movement of goods, information, and people.

What one may not realize, however, is how ingrained company/brand-specific consumption is in the lifestyles of both the legions of chaebol employees and the Korean citizenry at large. An example of "company life," as vividly described by Woo-Cumings:

The typical Hyundai worker drives a Hyundai car, lives in a Hyundai apartment, gets his mortgage from Hyundai credit, gets health care from a Hyundai hospital, sends his children to school on Hyundai loans or scholarships, and eats his meals at Hyundai cafeteria. If his son graduates out of the blue-collar work force and enters the ranks of well-educated technocratic professionals (which is the goal of every Korean parent), he may well work for Hyundai research and development. (2001, p. 370)

Despite not being a chaebol employee, I was not exempt from this brand-conscious existence while living in Korea. I have lived in a block of Hyundai Apartments that are typically constructed with Hyundai goods by Hyundai (or a closely affiliated partner). Similarly, my friends lived in other chaebol apartment blocks, such as Daewoo or Samsung. Though it was not obvious at first, I realized I was brushing my teeth with LG toothpaste and eating Samsung peanut butter once I read the fine print on the labels. Employees of any of the chaebols made sure to use an LG cell phone if they worked for LG, even though they expressed such sentiments as, "I would prefer the Samsung one," with a nod and a wink. In essence, consumption habits in Korea have been intrinsically tied to employment and identity due to the nature of chaebol life.

One may imagine, then, at a time when the lives of even greater numbers of the Korean populace were completely tied to chaebol life, how this existence was turned on its head on a large scale with the massive layoffs of the "IMF Crisis." The financial crisis was highly visible, but the social fallout was perhaps more severe because of how it shook the meanings of work and everyday life.

## AJEOSSIS THROUGH ADVERSITY

*The mothers and fathers generation, they would say, "you are the first generation that doesn't have to worry about food." After the economic base and infrastructure, they need something to enjoy. Not just American pop music, not just American movies. Pop music was gaining popularity from 1988. American AOL kind of time, and through that setting, men and women could meet and fall in love in that setting.*

—Michael

Returning to my encounter with the Ajeossi who owned the PC bang at the beginning of this chapter, I wish to now draw attention to how the dialogue in that PC bang indicated the very factors that led to the rise of online gaming in Korea. As a result of "tens of thousands of lost jobs and company bankruptcies" (Jin, 2011, p. 45) during the 1997 economic crisis, those employed by the financial sector along with everyone else, needed to deal with their new circumstances.

Suddenly without the all-encompassing support that came with company life, many found themselves alone, with little choice but to find a way to become entrepreneurs of one sort or another in order to survive. The number of individual stock investors alone increased from 1.32 million in 1997 to 3.97 million in 2002 (Jin, 2010, p. 23). Moreover, the PC bangs gave these stock investors the means to check on their investments without the need to subscribe to broadband services at home.

As other work on Internet cafés have shown, such as Wakeford's (2003) in London spaces, the PC bang in the Korean context afforded many different types of activity. For entrepreneurs at that point, it presented an opportunity to start a business fulfilling an unmet need of connectivity (Jin & Chee, 2008). For those who were unemployed and between jobs, the PC bang served as a substitute "office" for people to go to every day and night. Some of these people had not told their families about the change in circumstances. For youth, it was a place to access computers and games, and to socialize in between school, cram schools (hagwons), and home life.

## DOMINATION OF PC GAMING IN KOREA

Due to Korea's colonization by Japan in the early twentieth century, as well as its longstanding concern with Japanese cultural invasion, the Korean government had until 1998 banned Japanese cultural products, which included console games, films, and music. With the ban lifted, Korea gradually opened the market to Japanese culture, phasing in previously black market products, with console games from Japan making their public appearance in the Korean marketplace by 2002 (Lee, 2002).

As discussed earlier, the historical tension between the two countries has proven persistent and difficult to surmount (Hjorth & Chan, 2009; Jin & Chee, 2008). For example, Japanese companies who anticipated large profits in the Korean game market found that the endeavor generated disappointing revenue results (Jin, 2010, p. 50). With Japanese console makers such as Sony, Nintendo, and Sega experiencing difficulties penetrating the Korean market, Korean firms found an opportunity to develop their own domestic game industry.

While this explanation for the low console use in Korea is completely illogical in terms of the merit of the games, cultural and historical factors determined technology choice in Korea for many gamers.

## EDUCATION, LITERACY, AND EFFECTS OF PRIORITIZING STEM

In Korea, the messages that education is the highest virtue and value one can attain are ubiquitous. Though global economic market trends would include Korea in limitations to the linkages between education and mobility, education has been and still is a priority investment for most citizens. Michael Seth's (2002) examination of educational development in Korea notes that this has been central to its transformation in the latter part of the twentieth century. Indeed, an examination of how Koreans regard education provides insight into "the nation's rapid economic, social, and political transformation" (2002, p. 7). Attainment of formal education has been the one thing that most Koreans could control in a chaotic heap of other variables. After all, formal education has been the dominant currency by which families have sought to distinguish themselves in the hopes for greater social mobility. The narrative of the bootstrapped individual is common Korean lore and celebrated. Working in tandem with Confucian ideals for education, one may find self-made lawyers like the sixteenth president of Korea, Roh Moo Hyun, who came from very humble beginnings as the youngest son of a farmer. He was part of what Koreans call the "386 generation" who (at the time of inventing the term) were known for being a politically active group in their thirties, who went to university in the 1980s and were born in the 1960s. His generation was also the first generation to grow up in the most upwardly mobile and prosperous era, becoming the decision-making elite of the country. What is more, Koreans spend the largest share of their income on education globally (Seth, 2002). While I navigated the streets amidst the throngs of buses shuttling students from regular sessions of school, to hagwon, to another hagwon, it was plain to me that an inexhaustible public and private appetite for education, along with the opportunities it afforded was very much alive in the information-centric twenty-first century.

In order to improve Korea's economy, the government prioritized STEM disciplines (science, technology, engineering, mathematics). While this prioritization occurred at the expense of investment in the critical social sciences and humanities (Seth, 2002), these initiatives contributed to the growth in the industrial and informational capacities of its domestic workforce such that the nation is a global contender where STEM is concerned, has a strong export economy, as well as a veritable hotbed of technological activity due to its domestic talent. "No nation spends a larger share of its income on education" (Seth, 2002, p. 5).

## THE GLOBAL GAMES INDUSTRY

During my 2004 fieldwork, after only a month in Korea, I was invited by an American games publisher to participate in a "business matching" conference jointly held by Korean government agencies with the intention of finding global publishers for game developers. Through my voluntary participation in facilitating these dialogues and partnerships, I learned first hand from the Korean company representatives that Korea was utterly saturated with games and game development talent, which was why they were reaching out in their attempts to export games through global partnerships.

At various points throughout the years of researching online games in Korea and participating in government/industry games functions akin to those discussed above, I have formed numerous relationships in those sectors. With the conferences, workshops, and casual meet-up events acting as the essential "introductions" needed to transact in Korean culture, I was able to nurture these friendship/business networks, and naturally, these assisted greatly in my access to knowledgeable and high-ranking informants who have played a large role in shaping the insights I share in this work.

## MILITARY EXEMPTION POLICY

*Some of the entertainers in Korea—some singers, they do service and finally it was revealed that they were not working for the company. It's one way of escaping military service.*

*—Michael*

As contentious as the issues surrounding military service have been, military service for men in Korea is compulsory. At some point in one's late teens or early twenties, one is expected to give up over two years to this service, which is highly regarded and looked upon as a major transition to male adulthood. So much so that in job applications, one receives advantages over other candidates in the form of extra "points" and/or consideration for having completed military service. Even celebrities are officially not exempt, and in my interviews/discussions, people cited the saying, loosely translated, "Only a god can escape military service." The links to military service and the games industry became all the more apparent as my fieldwork went on, and also inform my subsequent focus on gender dynamics in the game industry later on in this book.

Michael imparted to me his first-hand knowledge regarding the military exemption policy:

*Florence: So I heard that if you are in a technical university that you can escape military service?*

*Subject: Yeah. There is a way. Middle-sized companies, they can have some specific number of spaces for Ministry of Service. It is not real service, [but a] kind of artistic way of military service. Most of them are programmers. Game programmers, they work for the company for three years and then their service is done.*

*S: I work with those . . . with those who serve military at the game company. And they . . . applied through their . . .*

*F: Ah, network.*

*S: Yeah.*

*F: So is it like a personal favor?*

*S: mm mm . . . <nod>*

Military service presents a break in a Korean male's otherwise rather linear trajectory of life and career development that males elsewhere may not face, and this has implications for the way in which they use online games as a medium of communication. There are a few exceptions to which my informants drew my attention. That is, for talented programmers and engineers accepted into competitive university programs there is a policy that exempts them from military duty, provided they stay in the country for five years. According to the 2010 Business Higher Education Forum STEM report (BHEF, 2010, p. 4), 15.6 percent of Bachelor's degrees in the US were awarded in the STEM disciplines, compared with 37.8 percent in South Korea. The military service exemption policy makes majoring in these STEM disciplines quite attractive and though not solely responsible for the prominence of game development talent, might suggest additional considerations for the pervasiveness of online game culture.

## GOVERNMENT POLICY AND INDUSTRY

> *The Korean gaming industry has been marked [by controversy] more than the film industry and drama and construction. Needed, the Ministry of Information and Culture, they all say culture is the key—Film, Games Industry—that Korea has to focus on. The day after, they stand against Internet and games.*
>
> —Michael

From a global and local industry standpoint, the dynamics between Korean business and technology policy has presented some fruitful outcomes as well as challenges. On the one hand, state-guided infrastructural initiatives have been instrumental in providing the conditions for success of the Korean online games industry (Jin, 2010, 2011; Oh & Larson, 2011). On the other hand, according to my informants, there are distinct challenges in what some in the industry may regard as too much interference, censorship, and micromanagement (such as government demanding that games companies adhere to online curfews or setting development timelines back to accommodate a certain level of violence or gore). This has been especially frustrating to a young industry that has become accustomed to blazing trails and high levels of social and economic mobility relative to older, more established ones.

It is likely that one might find a bit of cognitive dissonance when it comes to the discourse in and around the Korean online gaming technoscape. On the one hand, due to its prominent role in the Korean economy, the government supports online gaming through promotion, facilitation, and sponsorship of its glamorous events. On the other hand, it also sponsors Internet and online game addiction centers that are charged with the mission of curbing online game play.

In my interview with a government-industry manager, when discussing the trade minister responsible for online games, we talked about the economic drivers of such a seemingly contradictory policy stance. Having been born during the Korean War, the Minister was not terribly interested in games, but,

> *He changed his mind when he saw that the Korean video gaming industry is almost 50 percent larger than the Korean movie industry. Looking at that, they started thinking wow . . . this might work. Last year, 2008, we exported something like more than $1 billion worth of [online] games all over the world.*

An example of a recent industry/policy clash has been termed the "Cinderella" or "shutdown law," which prohibits those under sixteen years of age from playing online games from midnight to 6 a.m. (Yoon, 2011). The policy was initially conceived of as a strategy to curb online game addiction, but has not exhibited any effectiveness in the months following its implementation in late 2011. There are several reasons for this, which link back to youth online habits. First, the need to log onto websites in Korea using one's National Identification Number (NIN) was circumvented long ago for doing sundry tasks ranging from pornography to the online grocery shopping which a number of expats wished to do. Those who are underage would simply use fake numbers or those of family members, rendering the prohibition ineffective. Second, the law only applies to select games oriented toward younger audiences, and not the most popular ones. Third, the law might have actually backfired and driven any activity by young people further underground. The unintended consequences are numerous for a law that was initially intended to exhibit a governmental proactive stance when it came to issues of Internet addiction.

## ONLINE HABITS AND LIFESTYLES IN TANDEM

*I don't need to go to the bank all the time because I can use the Internet. I can buy things over the Net, I don't have to go to stores all the time. More than 50 percent of what I purchase is through the Internet. Diapers, everything. Negatively [blushing], I'm a gamer . . .*

—Seoul resident, middle-aged male

This chapter provided the reader with an idea of the complex foundations upon which online gaming came to be built in Korea. It also highlighted the mediating role of social relations, including notions of Confucianism, recent pivotal events in Korea's global history, and the continuing struggles within.

Understanding a nation by examining one dimension of its development is problematic in and of itself, without modeling one's own technological policies and development in the hopes of replicating such rapid adoption and prosperity. I seek to argue that above and beyond the context of technology and policy, it is imperative to closely look at the social conditions in this specific rise of technology use in order to gain a more complete picture of the specificities of Korea's transformation to learn: what is/is not replicable, and what should not be replicated.

Having experienced household life while living in Seoul, it was plain to me that the relative convenience of doing things over the Internet coincided with many incentives: sites enabled online ordering of groceries and general household items along with free delivery to homes. To a number of Koreans I observed and talked with, a notable benefit for them was that they could be more selective about when to go out into the press of overcrowded urban environments, which are often noisy and unpleasant. For the resident Korean population, the domestic conveniences of broadband-enabled services are numerous.

Not just to do with convenience, the everyday affordances of the Internet act in tandem with the prominence of PC gaming. It is also important to note the history of censorship and relatively recent restrictions on live performance culture, which included the cancellation of performances not deemed appropriate (for any reason, including being foreign) (Republic of South Korea, 2001). Laws such as the "Public Performance Act" have influenced the attitudes regarding possibilities for entertainment choices in Korea. Online gaming has thus provided an opportunity for people to partake in communal activities in public spaces in the form of eSports spectatorship, PC bangs, and the like.

## THE ELEPHANT IN THE ROOM

Naturally, it would not be ethnographic fieldwork without more taboo/uncomfortable topics brought up by informants. Many academic Internet studies do not discuss the role of pornography due to persistent taboos, though prominent scholarship by Susanna Paasonen, Alex Halavais, and a growing number of scholars has been key in bringing these issues to the fore through interdisciplinary points of engagement. To ignore the impact this aspect has had on the social shaping of these technologies, specifically, would be to provide a less complete picture and misrepresent human behavior online (Halavais, 2006). As broadband access has played a major role in the adoption of PC gaming in Korea, it has also fostered a whole set of other activities in tandem. During a more candid moment of my interview with Michael, he expressed the viewpoint that pornography and games of many types (gambling, casual, MMORPG, etc.) should be thought of as part of one technocultural landscape carved out by similar affordances.

> S: *Kind of like AOL, HiTel, or KT, Koreans spend time online . . . Online games were popular . . . and another thing was nudity-type things.*
>
> F: *Oh, pornography?*
>
> S: *Yeah. That was a major driver. Users get together in an Internet café, and that was how the public was exposed to broadband. Download, what would take*

*overnight, in less than an hour. Of course it is illegal, like music, but . . . that time, Internet was a big entertainment feature.*

In terms of what contributed to the popularity of online culture, he naturally pointed to the nation's broadband penetration rate, along with advertising and aggressive promotion of what can be done with the Internet to the general public.

Michael noted that gambling games also played a prominent role in creating user demand for Internet services.

*Another thing that made Korean online games successful was Internet bubble time was in Korea at the same time . . . Internet starts with Hangame. The Korean game; poker kind of game. Hangame was the first one to try that kind of experiment.*

Unlike Hangame, Korean portals like the recommendation-based search engine Naver and Daum community portals only focused on improving their advertising models and did not experience the same level of success, though Naver attempted to use Adwords before Google.

*Hangame did well with free games but at that time Hangame that was the only way we have to go. Otherwise we have to find another one.*

Indeed, the overarching culture, social structure, infrastructure, and policy galvanize to reinforce gaming and its place in mainstream Korean culture, as I shall discuss in the following chapter.

## NOTES

1. Policy, in the Korean use, often implies more of an "action" or "plan" than a rule/law.
2. For comparison's sake, that is equivalent to three times the area of Vancouver Island.

*Chapter 3*

# The Social Addict
## *Infrastructures of Togetherness*

*"So we're going tonight?" I asked, in a text message to Han. "Ye ye. See you at the subway station. Exit 2."*

Tonight was going to be all about a games tournament and I was excited. Han said I would be able to meet and talk with his good friends there, a couple of whom were self-described online game addicts.

Once I got myself to the station to meet Han, we walked to a coffee shop to meet with one of his best friends from high school, with whom I could chat about his online gaming habits. Over coffee, we were able to chat casually, and then do a longer interview with the questions I had prepared for gamers, to which Han's friend responded with enthusiasm and, at times, confusion. I started to get an idea of what was appropriate to ask in the Korean context, and which questions simply did not seem to apply here.

Clearly, the Internet café research I had done in North America could not just be rehashed here. After a while, another friend joined us and we all left together for some pre-games dinner.

We showed up for dinner at a barbeque restaurant. We took off our shoes at the front and shuffled across the laminate floor, through the greasy blue smoke permeating the air from the other tables, to sit at one of many large rectangular tables. As we waited for the other friends to show up, the Ajumma brought bottles of water, plastic cups, colorful side dishes, and soju. One by one, our table filled with friends who pulled up their cushions to the casual feast. I was definitely the outsider in so many ways, but particularly because these were friends who were in a collective "inner circle," having known one another often since primary school. Their level of comfort with one another was clear, in their ease of interaction. Despite my status as the outsider, Han's introduction to the group allowed me instant rapport, and save for a few moments of shyness, my foreign presence seemed promptly forgotten and replaced by the bustle of the smoking, crackling, popping of cooking meat along with calls of *"ONE SHOT!"*

After everyone paid their share of 10,000KRW for dinner, a couple of the fellows had an intense craving for ice cream to offset the spicy meat and kimchi. So, all of us went to the corner grocery store and bought either cigarettes or frozen confections from the Ajeossi. Standing outside the shop smoking or eating ice cream, we chatted and then gradually made our way to the PC bang.

"We are here!" Han announced. The PC bang was quite nondescript, with a small lit sign indicating its presence in B1 (basement level). We trudged down a flight of steep stairs, and opened a frosted glass door to a veritable emporium of PCs in rows, games posters and paraphernalia, a couple zone, and a snack bar.

Being relatively early in the evening post-dinner, we were able to commandeer an entire section for our "LAN party." This had been what I was waiting for. I was excited to play with a large group of self-described "game addicts" in Korea and got ready for a rousing night of participant observation with StarCraft, which I had experience playing from when it first came out in North America years prior.

As my Terran base was destroyed quicker each time, it became clear that I was clearly outmatched. I was a bit disappointed how quickly the game was over for me, even though I had braced myself for "pwnage." Not to be put off, I took the opportunity to observe the others as they yelled their intentions back and forth, joking and trash talking.

I also spent time observing activity in other parts of the PC bang, and playing other games when Han or the others opted out of a round.

From experience as well as what I had been told, going from place to place throughout the night (as opposed to just sitting in one place for dinner, dessert, etc.) provides the chance for people to excuse themselves from the outing and go home or to some other engagement. To leave in the middle of a "round" would typically be considered less polite. After the group had their fill of gaming, we all went to a chicken baengi. In a bright yellow and blue stall, we sat down on stools around pitchers of Cass beer and a couple of mounds of fried chicken. This was the time when stories from military service were traded and those who were not yet attached could be playfully jibed about not having found girlfriends yet. As it was still a "work night" for those in the party with employment, the night wound to a conclusion and we said our goodbyes.

"Text me when you get home so I know you're OK." Han shouted after me.

I did not fully realize it at the time, but that was the night years ago that my network in Korea truly exploded.

## CHAPTER OVERVIEW

To call gaming an addiction is to woefully misrepresent the prominent role this medium plays in the everyday life and culture in Korea. Having discussed factors that laid the foundation for the rise of games, this chapter now shifts gears to examine specific instances of how gaming interacts with the local culture, social structure, and infrastructure. The insights in this chapter are informed by my fieldwork in Korea.

The online gaming culture that has evolved in Korea for the last decade has been fascinating for me as an ethnographer. The megacity of Seoul, where I spent the majority of my time in the country, has been an especially rich and dynamic site for this research. I consider myself most fortunate to have been present at various crucial moments in its evolution, partaking in overwhelming spectacle, and experiencing the mundane minutiae of navigating everyday life.

Through the narratives I collected from others as well as through the process of reckoning with my own reality of living and operating within Korean power structures for an extended period of time, I became sensitized to three main themes: (1) culture, (2) social structure, and (3) infrastructure. To phrase things in terms of McLuhan, these three themes encompassed what I wish to state about the occurrence of gaming as a Figure on Korean Ground. By far the most complicated work has been in the weaving of ethnographic insight with understanding the local media ecology. This chapter is indeed the richest and rewarding to write for bringing my original contribution to readers, as I could not have obtained these insights without having been deeply engaged with local residents in this particular Korean context.

## CULTURE

This chapter describes how people navigated the cultural intricacies of their day-to-day lives, where online gaming and technology in general figured prominently.

Why has gaming been the object of derision much like other forms of media controversies? In the end, is the distinction (a la Bourdieu) (1984) between what is a real and important communication medium merely a subjective judgment based upon high/low culture and ideology? For example, why is a sport like golf typically met with respect, but online gaming met with strange looks and chuckles? As Williams writes (Attallah, 2002; Williams, 1974), aesthetic judgments as to what constitutes "good" and "bad" have been known to create hierarchical relationships between the culture of the affluent and the culture of the working classes and those hierarchies replicate and prescribe how people act within these institutions. Unlike most other places in the world, games are not merely the province of a stereotypically marginal community in Korea. As indicated by games scholars focusing on Korea (Hjorth & Chan, 2009; Jin & Chee, 2008; Jin, 2010, p. 60), online games shine in the spectacle of Korean mainstream mass culture in the form of television shows, celebrities, and as an everyday activity that intersects pursuits of work and leisure.

At present, the PC bang is a gathering place where youth do a wide range of social activities such as meet friends, have dates, or blow off steam from a demanding school day. These emergent practices that toggled between online and offline spaces were very intriguing in how these spaces resembled Venn diagrams more than spheres of existence that were separate from one another. In the couple zones of PC bangs, sharing a loveseat with one's date could be done while playing StarCraft, instant messaging, or shopping online. The PC bang could serve as a meeting place for an hour or two between schooling, or as a rallying point between activities during the night. Even in the hours while the subway system closed, one could find a comfortable spot in a leather chair at a computer, surf the Web, sleep, or eat something until daylight.

Second, there is a celebrity culture surrounding professional gamers, who have very lucrative (albeit relatively short) careers in online game competitions. This activity is often referred to as pro-gaming or eSports (Jin, 2010; Taylor, 2012). South Korea's mainstream game culture became especially known internationally when game players like Guillaume Patry, moved from his home in Canada to South Korea specifically for the chance to make a living competing in these online game tournaments.

In a now classic interview with Geartest.com, he confirmed that he was living the dream of many aspiring eSports athletes: he was winning thousands of dollars every tournament, dating supermodels, rubbing shoulders with celebrities who also played video games, and gaining acceptance for his gaming in Korea when he could not elsewhere.

> "There are 25,000 PC game rooms ['bangs'] in South Korea. It started out with pool, then karaoke, and five years ago, game rooms," Guillaume said as he explained South Korean gaming culture. "In high schools, everyone knows who's best in math and StarCraft." The rankings for StarCraft are posted right next to the academic results in South Korean schools, he said.
>
> Guillaume's eyes light up when he describes the difference between the popular acceptance of gaming in South Korea compared to the rest of the world. Outside of South Korea, gaming as a profession is largely unknown, and gaming is often viewed as something for socially maladjusted teenage boys, he says. In South Korea it's a different story. (Geartest.com, 2004)

While the number of PC bangs have since dwindled due to the emergence of Wi-Fi at coffee shops and increased portability of sophisticated personal computing devices, this interview is still particularly enlightening for why Korea is a particularly compelling case for the study of mainstream online gaming culture. These events problematize the dogmatic categories of online and offline, as the gaming culture in Korea clearly illustrates the porous nature of those boundaries.

Third, I attempt to theorize the interpersonal dynamics afforded by the role technology plays in the Korean cultural landscape. In his book *Understanding Media: The Extensions of Man* (1994), McLuhan employs the Greek myth of Narcissus as a metaphor to describe what happens to someone experiencing the extension of themselves afforded by a particular medium.

According to McLuhan, the myth is powerful for how it illustrates the fascination men [sic] feel, "by any extension of themselves in any material other than themselves" (McLuhan, 1994, p. 41). This is exemplified in Korean media ecology by the youth that can be found communicating by way of online gaming avatars (Pearce et al., 2009), their Cyworld minihompys (a Korean social networking site predating Facebook), and doing any variety of activities on their mobile phones, which are increasing in prominence through smartphone usage.

McLuhan uses the Greek myth of Narcissus to talk about the numbness reflected in "narcosis." The myth explains that the youth was so captivated by his own reflection in the water because he thought it to be another person. He stayed there so long he grew roots, and that gave us the Narcissus flower that grows beside water in the present day. McLuhan connects this myth with his own media theory in that this extension of himself by this mirror numbed his perceptions until he became the "servomechanism of his own extended or repeated image" (McLuhan, 1994, p. 41). This concept is also discussed at length in Onufrijchuk (1998). Once Narcissus adapted to the extension of himself, he became a closed system. With such a myth directly concerned with a fact of human experience, the metaphor of Narcissus seems the beginning of a more reasonable explanation for the heavy use of media than its typical dismissal as a medical "addiction." The millennial generation (Pew Research Center, 2010) has particularly been publicly criticized for their "narcissism," and exhibitionism in their use of online media (Conger, 2011). Yet, it would be unfortunate to accept this label without an understanding of possible theories of media use.

Cognizant of—as well as having observed—the types of pressure Korean youth are under in matters of educational achievement (Seth, 2002) and familial expectations, I gravitated toward this theoretical understanding of this environment that, to me, resembled a pressure cooker. In my candid conversations with Korean parents, they would often bemoan the state of education in Korea as being too achievement oriented, how they were spending too much money on supplementary schooling, and how things might be different for their children without the competition parents feel amongst each other regarding their children's achievement. From the point of view of those embroiled in the system, being shuttled from lesson to lesson, any relief from the pressure cooker system, however brief, would be savored amidst an overall ethos of "just survive." The "numbness" of Narcissus that McLuhan describes presents an alternative understanding for media use that places the user at the heart of a type of social "shock." "For if Narcissus is numbed by his self-amputated image, there is a very good reason for the numbness. ". . . A person suddenly deprived of loved ones and a person who drops a few feet unexpectedly will both register shock" (McLuhan, 1994, p. 44). He maintains that shock induces a generalized numbness or an increased threshold to all types of perception, and, as a result the "victim" of this shock seems immune to pain or sense.

McLuhan asserts that it is the Narcissus-style continuous embrace of our own technology in daily use that places the user in a role of subliminal awareness and numbness in facing the extension of ourselves. As a consequence, people easily become servomechanisms of the very technologies of which they feel in control.

When a person extends oneself, there is a resultant amplification in the sense of that extension. The Narcissus myth accounts for the numbness of blocking of perception as a type of self-defense mechanism to allow the nervous system to bear such amplification and extension. McLuhan argues that Narcissus' image is a self-amputation or extension induced by "irritating pressures." However, as a counter-irritant, the image in turn produces a generalized numbness or shock unrecognizable to Narcissus. "Self-amputation forbids self-recognition" (McLuhan, 1994, p. 43).

McLuhan then attempts to draw further parallels between the nervous system and media use. He posits that the body, as a group of sustaining and protective organs for the central nervous system, serves as a buffer against sudden variations of stimulus in one's environment. He goes on to say that sudden social failure or shame is a shock that some may "take to heart" or that may cause muscular disturbance in general, signaling for the person to withdraw from the threatening situation (McLuhan, 1994). As pseudoscientific as this line of reasoning may seem, it does pose a reasonable metaphor for the social reasons as to why people may "retreat" into unhealthy or destructive forms of media use. It is therefore interesting to explore how these concepts may apply to the examination of online gaming in everyday Korean life in this chapter.

## SOCIAL STRUCTURE

Does Neo-Confucianism affect the Korean technocultural environment, and if so, how? In a Confucian society such as Korea's, age is privileged. The games industry is somewhere that Korean youth can, and have, thrived. This success is indicative of how age and class structures are regarded in Korea and are worth exploring here by integrating considerations of national culture and policy with media industries as in Chung (2008, 2021). John Lie's critical work on the political economy of Korea asserts that, "there was nothing obvious or predictable about the path of South Korean development. It is a singular story that cannot be explained by any general theory of national development and offers no simple model for other developing countries" (Lie, 1998, p. viii). This aspect is important to consider as other countries examine Korean models for direct application to their own national policies (Oh & Larson, 2011, p. xiv).

First, family home dynamics in Korean cities necessitate that the majority of socialization occurs outside the home. Privacy is at a premium. This has given rise to the "bang culture" (room culture), which facilitates activities away from the home, and away from critical prying eyes of family.

Second, online games as a medium of communication, serve as a hierarchy leveler. This is akin to playing a round of golf with the boss, but in most cases being allowed to beat the boss. Cases as found in Feenberg's (1995, p. 198) examination of Kawabata's famous novel *The Master of Go*, which vividly details how gaming and social structure intersect—that a person's social rank colors the interactions on and off the gameboard (or on and off the playing field as the case may be). It is an interesting parallel in this case and in the Korean context, presents implications for age and class mobility as I examine the fluidity of online and offline interactions in that context.

Third, gaming has provided an economically convenient activity for Korean youth, for whom there is a limited set of affordable leisure activities. Due to the low cost of PC bangs at about $1 an hour they work well with student budgets when even a visit to the coffee shop costs at least $2 or more. These activities have also given rise to young people's literacy in computer games, technological literacy, and dreams of careers in the domestic games industry including the possibility of gaming at a professional level. As mentioned earlier, these opportunities were more likely in Korea than any other country in the world. With the rise in mobile and wireless games, the PC bangs have dwindled, though the need and function for game-ful spaces has not. One may bring their laptops or mobile devices to shared areas that keep pace with the general level of mobility and play that permeates the user base.

According to the Organisation for Economic Co-operation and Development (OECD) figures, Korea is number one in the world for time spent at work. This has immense implications for how communication technology is used, as work and play are blurred. Indeed, workers in South Korea have the longest work hours in the world. The average South Korean works 2,390 hours each year, according to the OECD. This is over four hundred hours longer than the next longest-working country and 34 percent more hours than the average in the United States (1,777). In Canada, the average of hours worked per year is 1,717. An average workweek in South Korea is forty-four hours or longer. Many people start their day at 8 a.m. and end at around 7 p.m. or later, often having dinner before returning to work. Until legislation in 2004 that virtually abolished the six-day workweek in large corporations, Korea was the only country in the OECD that worked Saturdays. South Korea and Japan are the only countries where death by work, or "kwarosa" (Hangul: 과로사) or "karoshi" respectively, is a recognized phenomenon.

The interaction between work and play has been significant in Korean culture, particularly from agrarian traditions like flying kites between toiling in farmer's fields. It would appear highly likely, given my experience with Korean work days that the seamlessness between work and play practices has contributed to the notion that Koreans are particularly addicted to gaming due to hours clocked. Compared to Calvinist notions of the separate nature of work and leisure, the Korean practices of interspersing the personal with the professional appears rather normalized. My most recent experiences immersed in large Korean game company culture, however, indicate some important movements toward increased support of family time and recognition of their role in diversity, equity, and inclusion in their operations (Chee, Hjorth, & Davies, 2021).

## INFRASTRUCTURE/POLICY

South Korea has achieved the highest broadband penetration in the world through deliberate investment initiatives. It is one of the most densely populated nations in the world, with 10 million living in Seoul (and 25 million living in the National Capital Area), out of 50 million within a 100,210 square kilometer area. Much of the terrain is hyper-urban, and green space is scarce as is general public space. Internet cafes, malls, and other commodified meeting places compensate for the scarcity of community space.

This section discusses findings associated with the infrastructural affordances of online gaming in Korea, and potential policy implications arising from the investigation. First, as the previous chapter on the rise of Korean gaming explicates, there were many contributing factors that created the current information infrastructure in contemporary Korea. It is not only the information infrastructure that is of note, but how people navigate the everyday instances of this infrastructure as it intertwines with the previous sections of culture and social structure. Second, I shall discuss how these spatial factors (modern urbanity) and social upheaval have been leveraged in ways that are not readily apparent to a cursory analysis of online gaming in Korea. Family, economic, and geopolitical pressures (to name a few) all provide insight into the function of gaming vis a vis a type of McLuhanesque retribalization. Third, the various strategies and patterns of youth as they move through these technologies shall be discussed as the chapter wraps up.

## KOREAN GAMERS AND SOCIALITY

Alongside a growing awareness and respect for media scholarship has been the proliferation of work decrying the displacement of a greater public welfare, health, civic engagement (Putnam, 2000), and general well-being by one form of electronic media such as the television (Postman, 1985). The online video game has garnered much attention as a potentially "dangerous" and diabolically "addictive" medium (Clark & Scott, 2009). Analyses that focus on the specific medium more than the environment in which it interfaces with people largely obscure the bigger picture of how societies respond to electronic media and act upon knee-jerk suppositions and scapegoating in lieu of even more difficult discussions surrounding education pressure (Korea) and gun control (United States). The nature of games and the study of the social dynamics thereof continue to grow in concert with technological advancement. However, decades later, the tendencies toward convenient explanations remain at a point that, for better or worse, the theorizing requires less updating than one might hope.

One may note this trend in other forms of media such as print, but most notably television in communication studies. Joshua Meyrowitz (1985) asserted that because of electronic media, physical location no longer plays an important role in shaping our experiences and behaviors, nor does the physical presence of people "with" us. Although Meyrowitz concentrated primarily on television, his work is typical of a particular perspective that sees the impact of electronic media on society as unidirectional as opposed to mutually co-constituted.

## GLOBAL VILLAGE: THE END OF SPACE IN NETWORKED SOCIETIES?

Cultural artifacts such as television or video games can have different ascribed meanings depending on cultural context. Throughout this thesis, one may see how the matters of physical and cultural embodiment do indeed matter. We are not, as some would wish, "post-geographical" nor have national borders become less important. One might argue that national divisions play an even larger role in differentiating our modes of production in vastly different contexts and media ecologies. For example, the role played by access to social media in revolution, and uneven consequences for data and privacy violations abound. As Franklin (1999) asserts throughout her work, technologies are developed and used within particular social, economic, and political contexts.

In my own work that now spans the histories of Web 1.0, Web 2.0 with social media, and now Web3, I have championed the need to assess the culture in which media is created and the context in which it is used in order to arrive at valuable insights about people's experiences. As digital games are increasingly recognized as a growing pastime and mode of social expression, it becomes that much more crucial to contribute to the dialogue regarding the interplay between technology and the development of human relationships.

Brian Sutton-Smith (1997, p. 120) has asserted: "Playing games for the sake of games is always playing games for the sake of games in a particular social context with its own particular social arrangements. There is no lasting social play without play culture." His work has been notable for putting forward the view that the rhetoric of a larger culture will have its own socializing influence, and the norms and hierarchies of the gaming society and general society will interpenetrate the game with its own particular social arrangements. Phrased another way, in order to assess the longevity and sustainability of social play, it is important to look at the specific context and historical circumstances of the culture in which that play is situated. In the Korean case, it is very much the case that contrary to general media portrayal and popular belief at global and local levels, the reasons for participating in online gaming are diverse, many of which go beyond the games in and of themselves. The reasons implicate a whole host of sociocultural factors that I have and will point out in this chapter.

## FIGURES ON KOREAN GROUND

In the early 2000s when I commenced this research, the studies of technology and society as they interfaced with games as a medium of communication were still relatively obscure given the lack of prominence in major mainstream communication publication venues and conferences. For example, the now internationally prominent Association of Internet Researchers (AoIR), of which I became a member in 2003, had been founded in the United States for about five years (officially since 1999). Though I was only starting graduate studies at that time, I found myself in community with those at the forefront of attempts to figure out how technologies have been affecting the daily lives of individuals within a society such as Korea's and vice versa. No longer able to remain aloof and dissociated in our global village, engagement with the exotic "others" of media has instead become deep engagement with global counterparts who may affect our daily lives on a regular basis more than even next-door neighbors might. Specifically, of research in the area of Korean media (Hjorth, 2006; Jin, 2011; Jouhki, 2008; Yoon, 2006) that included the perspectives found in studying the massive social upheaval being experienced on this particular Ground from cognate methodological standpoints. These discussions and collaborations were important for me and represented an innovative set of approaches for studying rapidly globalizing and localized media.

McLuhan showed his concern by noting that the new media and technologies that we use to amplify and extend ourselves constitute "huge collective surgery carried out on the social body with complete disregard for antiseptics" (1994, p. 64). Current media scholarship concerning Korea is only beginning to assess the social fallout inherent in a time of both mental and physical national flux, acceleration, and disruption.

Research on the appropriation of technology in Korea forces media scholars to study not only the content, but "the specific medium and cultural matrix within which the particular medium operates" (McLuhan, 1994, p. 11). That is, in this case, "form" trumps "content" and "the medium is the message." The technological Figures on South Korean Ground are of particular interest for this thesis, particularly because of the rapid transformation from a primarily agrarian, to industrial, to information economy that has only occurred within the last fifty years since the Korean War (1950–1953). In the last decade, the emergence of nationwide broadband Internet access has only quickened the pace of technological change in an already frenetically adapting sociocultural milieu. In many ways, youth have had to reimagine their communities in unprecedented ways.

## TOGETHERNESS IN CONTEXT

Most of the discourse surrounding addiction to technology, in the way video game players are viewed as "patients" to be drugged (Chee & Smith, 2005), or attendees at Internet addiction camps like the Korean "Jump Up Internet Rescue School" (Fackler, 2007), individualizes the relationship to the offending "substance" (or medium). This viewpoint comes at the expense of viewing the situation as a cluster of mediated social relations that facilitates human connection. As with many other communication technologies like television (Postman, 1985), online games have been regarded as frivolities, and users guilty of isolating themselves from "real" social interaction. Moreover, excessive media use has been implicated in a perceived lack of civic engagement, as in the case of American society written about by Putnam (2000).

This discourse privileges offline and established activities as the only means of true communication. One may observe this in the discourse of "virtual" versus "real" life, as it implies that online activities are somehow not real. Using what Feenberg and Bakardjieva (2004) asserted in their viewpoint that online communities are "imaginary" social constructs, I would say that in the Korean case, embodiment still persists and is creating community both online and offline, most often as one.

Prior to heading to Korea, I had conducted North American studies of gamer culture and what Vieta, Smith, and I called the "Interactional Self" (Chee, Vieta, & Smith, 2006). The sociological phenomenology forwarded by Alfred Schutz (Schutz, 1962/1966, 1970) argued that users are one self rather than separate, fragmented presences between the online and offline. Qualitative inquiries have done much to advance the perspective that online spaces present similar qualities to those of offline communal spaces (Wellman & Gulia, 1999), namely third places as termed by Oldenburg (1997) as used in Kendall (2002) and Steinkuehler and Williams (2006). According to Oldenburg (1997), third places are those places that are neither work nor home, but provide psychological comfort and support. Although he wrote about third places for and within a US context, similar parallels can be drawn for the importance of these third places in Korea and other national contexts. These are liminal spaces between online and offline worlds. This perspective is found in Nardi's field study of online gaming in Chinese Internet cafes (2010) as well as in Szablewicz (2010) and Lindtner and Szablewicz (2011). This chapter contributes to the argument that the culture associated with online gaming is inextricable from the offline cultures in which its users live.

## THE NUMBNESS OF NARCISSUS

McLuhan notes that technological innovations do not necessarily introduce absolutely new elements into human society, but may still accelerate and enlarge the scale of previous human functions which in turn create new lifestyles (work and leisure). In no other country has this acceleration been more concentrated and apparent than Korea. The pace of technological adoption, as evidenced by Koreans' many uses of information and communication technologies in their myriad forms, has served to create a sort of Narcissus-like numbness society-wide.

Perhaps the rapid social transformation in all aspects of material and social life has caused Koreans to cling even harder to the technologies implemented along its own path to the "Information Superhighway," a term which former US Vice President Al Gore has been credited with promoting in Korea during his official visits.

In a nation of nearly 50 million people, over half play online games in the form of popular MMORPGs like the iterations of World of Warcraft/Aion/Lineage,

RTS genres like StarCraft, or online poker/GoStop (which are also frequently counted as online games in statistical reports) (PricewaterhouseCoopers, 2006, 2007, 2008). This figure is overrepresented in proportion of population by the younger broadband Internet generation accustomed to these modes of communication. These same users also likely possess a mobile phone and Cyworld "minihompy," which is a personal profile webpage preceding the North American Facebook phenomenon by several years, but with similar multifaceted modes of social networking capabilities. In the last few years, Facebook profiles have gained in popularity, especially for Koreans who told me, "Cyworld is for Korean friends, Facebook is for foreign friends."

While it is easy to fall into the seductive trap of recounting the sheer numbers involved in the Korean social media and gaming users that one may observe in Hjorth (2006), it has been intriguing to consider what keeps this momentum of media use going in Korea. McLuhan's assertion is that various physical and social therapies are forms of communication, and whether they are physical or social, may serve as a counter-irritant that aids in the maintenance of equilibrium with the body's nervous system. Whereas pleasure in the form of recreation, such as sports, entertainment, or narcotics serves as a counter-irritant, an antidote for irritating forces, true comfort is the removal of irritants. "Both pleasure and comfort are strategies of equilibrium for the central nervous system" (McLuhan, 1994, p. 43), but when it is impossible to remove the irritant, people retreat into their reserves of counter-irritants. Along with that, "any invention or technology is an extension or self-amputation of our physical bodies, and such extension also demands new ratios or new equilibriums among the other organs and extensions of the body" (1994, p. 45). Korean youth are certainly dealing with many "irritating pressures" that may be driving them to the metaphorical side of the water in order to assume the same position of Narcissus staring at his mediated reflection. As I noted earlier, there is family pressure to be the top student in school (many youth are in some type of tutelage from sun up to sun down, every day), and general peer pressure to conform. I marveled at how aptly McLuhan described the stresses and pressures of the type that I encountered Korean youth operating both within and under while gaming: "And we often create artificial situations that rival the irritations and stresses of real life under controlled conditions of sport and play" (1994, p. 42). For example, the ubiquitous PC game rooms in Korea extend and expand upon the physical spaces and opportunities in which youth may engage with media or evoke a notion of community center. In most other places around the globe, PC game rooms and the chances to access broadband Internet are much harder to come by (Chee, de Castell, & Taylor, 2011). Thus, "it is the accumulation of group pressures and irritations that prompt invention and innovation as counter-irritants" (1994, p. 47). Using McLuhan's Narcissus as a metaphor, one may interpret the way

Korean youth have used these technologies to both ameliorate and perpetuate the various irritants that are only increasing in contemporary Korea.

## PC BANG CULTURE AND WHY GAMES ARE ANYTHING BUT ANTI-SOCIAL

The previous chapter pointed to how Korea's unique history, limited geographical area, and governmental support have encouraged the development of a sophisticated broadband infrastructure, gaming culture, and the PC bang. In this section, I will explain how the PC bang became a vital center of activity in Korean neighborhoods, serving many purposes, including compensating for services one would typically think belonged to other institutions.

Due to their relatively high numbers, PC bangs are highly competitive and cheaper than any other activity. Youth, with their limited incomes, often choose the PC bang as a place to commune, fulfilling the role of a "third place" (Oldenburg, 1997). These places often contain people of like minds and like interests. In Korea, such third places become especially important because entertaining one's friends is rarely done in the home due in large part to spatial and cultural reasons.

At a third place such as a PC bang, one can choose from a myriad of activities including online games, e-mail, online chat, Web surfing, visiting matchmaking sites, people watching, eating, smoking, being with big groups of friends, or just being with one's significant other in a warm and safe setting. A PC bang also has been known to be a cheap place for shelter in the middle of the night, or within the broader context of an unkind job market, a place for the unemployed to spend the day. Given these social dynamics, the PC bang is the site of numerous significant social interactions. Where other arguments (Kendall, 2002; Steinkuehler & Williams, 2006) concerning specific games suggest that MMORPGs and other online hangouts are a site that encompass behaviors warranting their categorizations as a "third place," I argue that the online games themselves are yet more of a "fourth place," especially when situated within the third places of PC bangs where embodiment still reigns as a chief determinant of action. Though there has been some debate about this conceptualization (Jonsson, 2010), the evidence I have encountered in the contextual studies I have carried out point out that the games themselves are often not the prime motivator for people to go to a PC bang, and engagement continues to be primarily determined by one's conditions of embodiment. There is no one single "cause" of excessive online gaming if one thinks of it as a means by which people communicate; nor are the reasons for the activity a universal, cross-cultural, physical "condition" diagnosable in biomedical terms.

As mentioned earlier, PC bangs are typically very popular as places to go because of their cheap rates and accessibility. Every neighborhood in Seoul averages about one PC bang per block. When one looks out at the cacophony of densely built structures, the ubiquitous PC bangs are easy to spot. It is interesting to note that the rate for PC bangs was substantially more expensive (about $10.00 US per hour) in the late 1990s. As availability and competition in PC bangs has increased, prices have decreased. In recent years, the rate has generally stabilized around the $1.00 (US) per hour mark, with some places offering discounts at non-peak times, with even greater discounts for "members." These rates are much more affordable to young people on a limited income than that of other, more expensive "bangs" with other activities, such as "norae bangs" (karaoke room), "DVD bangs" (movie watching room), or board game bangs, which are at least $2 to $3 more expensive per hour.

At the street level, one may often see multiple PC bangs within one building on different floors, indicated by flashing neon signs. "PC방" rarely exist on the first floor, as those are usually occupied by other businesses such as service shops. Thinking back to the times I would explore different PC bangs, I remember venturing up or down tiny, dingy, often dodgy looking stairs and passing through a tinted glass door with that little bit of trepidation and anxiety of what could possibly lay in wait, as I have learned over the years that the conditions are quite variable. At times the cafes can be composed of five computer stations, or more than a hundred with deluxe executive chairs. The air can be oppressively thick and blue with cigarette smoke, or clear and sweetly perfumed depending on the type of cafe.

The equipment may be old or state of the art. I have gone into "low-spec" cafes that favor MMORPGs with lower hardware requirements, and state-of-the-art cafes capable of running the latest games, such as FPS (first-person shooter) games. If the PC bang has adequate capacity, it may contain a specially demarcated "couple zone" in which the stations are two computers in front of a "couple chair," in the form of a loveseat or expanded chair without a separating armrest. The section, usually darker, is designed for dating couples in need of socially acceptable proximity bonding in a quasi-public environment. The general area may have a snack bar, varying in size. Standard items available tend to be oriented around basic sustenance, such as vitamin drinks, water, soft drinks, bags of chips, cookies, and instant noodle soup bowls (ramyun).

Upon entry, one can get a plastic card from the clerk at the front counter for paying by the hour, though in recent times PC bangs have favored memberships and payment tied to specific users while providing incentives like discounted or bulk hourly rates which have implications for security, data collection, and invoicing. At the computer, one will be prompted to enter either the card number, or more often than not, one's membership number in order to activate the billing time for that computer station. Especially perturbing to me as well as other foreigners was that many transactions online require a National Identification Number (NIN) to gain access to even the most basic Korean websites, including retail. Usually, this number presents greater convenience and less friction to Korean citizens, but to interlopers like myself, it was the difference between being self-sufficient and an "alien." Upon leaving, the clerk used to punch in the number of the card, and the tab was settled. This practice and the relative anonymity of that specific transaction has since changed to link subscription accounts, mobile numbers, and other identifying data.

## FUNCTION OF THE PC BANG

The PC bang in Korea has become an institution that serves a number of different purposes. By being open twenty-four hours a day, seven days a week, they serve functions that may compensate for shortcomings in needs fulfillment in other contexts. For example, according to Kym Stewart's fieldwork in Korean educational contexts (2004, p. 62), "The PC bang and bang culture in Korea . . . [provides] children with media use opportunities outside of their home, away from parental rules and regulations and among groups of friends, which does not often happen within the Korean homes." In my own field observations and interviews in Korea I have seen media use and less formal modes of interaction with a wider range of peers than might otherwise occur at home or school. The participation of young Koreans in online games represented one facet of a broader community and way of life.

That Korean youth spent their hours at PC bangs and associated spaces of liminality, I attempt to curate the reasons why, as they manifested and continue to emerge as signifiers of a broader, and deeper culture of play. Rather than dismiss the participants as "game addicts," I present a few examples of the various motives one might have for spending a lot of time gaming at PC game rooms or otherwise. It will become apparent that those motivations have very little to do with which game is on the screen.

## DOMESTIC PRESSURES

*Why would anyone want to see my home? It's like my closet.*

—Korean informant, middle aged, male

A particularly memorable gamer I interviewed was a university student in his late twenties, who made a point to say that he spent as much time outside of his home as possible and that his reasons for going to PC bangs were not just about the games. His everyday routine would be to go out to dinner with his friends; go to a PC bang in his neighborhood; and, while there, play a variety of games, including Lineage, StarCraft, and KartRider. Upon arriving home around midnight when his parents were asleep, he would go online in his room, and play for another few hours. One might assume that playing games in a PC bang meant that the player had no other access to computer games, but more often than not the players I encountered do have home computers. Why, then, would someone pay money to play the same games outside? The reasons range from exhibiting one's gaming skill, to various private/public behaviors in the form of online dating/gambling/day-trading, but a major reason this player cited was that he could smoke at PC bangs, whereas at home he could not, as his parents frowned upon that habit. Two major reasons were his lack of "comfort" in his own home and deliberate avoidance of encounters with his parents. Comfort, as he sees it, is most likely his ability to be himself amidst friends, smoke elsewhere, and escape the constraints of intergenerational friction he feels living with his parents. Although things are changing slowly to reflect Western models of behavior, it is still quite common for young Koreans to live with their parents until they are married. In fact, it is often expected. Thus many coping strategies, such as those talked about by other informants, are rather typical attitudes of youth living with their parents. For him as well as others, the PC bang was a way to escape the various familial constraints of his domestic environment.

Another informant actually talked about his lack of desire to play online games, but that he did so in order to spend time with his friends, which was further evidence that motivations do not rest solely on the desire to play games. One interviewee would go to the PC bang most weekdays after drinking and spend about three hours playing StarCraft, despite having access to good computers at home. He bemoaned the fact that he found the skill demands of StarCraft too difficult and that he really wanted to play simpler games if they were a condition of spending time with his friends. Whether they were "only casual," "recovering game addicts," or "not gamers," those I interviewed still spent time in PC bangs and reported spending at least an average of five hours per week in games in order to be with others and maintain bonds with their peer groups. As Sutton-Smith states, "It has been shown that sometimes players play primarily to be with others" (1997, p. 105), which coincides with Korean gaming culture as observed in this study.

Referencing their own multi-sited fieldwork experiences that include investigations in South Korea, Dourish and Bell indicate that homes are extremely private places (Dourish & Bell, 2011). Socializing is typically done outside the home, and in the Korean context my own fieldwork experiences have made it clear that there is much more reticence to treat the home as anything more than one's closet, with living conditions and family thoroughly exposed in close quarters. In contemporary Korea, it would be unorthodox and in many cases even unseemly to invite someone back to the home, especially under the critical gaze of elders.

## COURTSHIP

Online games have played a part in courtship for Korean youth. The PC bang infrastructure has helped many escape the constraints of family. I encountered many young couples using the game atmosphere in PC bangs to engage in courtship practices, and it was common to have "couple zones," which are separate areas specifically designated for couples. Sometimes these zones are dimly lit, with comfortable couple-oriented seating and PCs that are closer together. Though the PC bangs at present have more competition in this regard from an increasing number of coffee shops, free Wi-Fi, and a proliferation of personal laptops, the opportunities for courtship around game-specific play are significant.

One particularly memorable interview (Chee, 2006, p. 233) that centered upon this topic was with a female university student who told me she had been playing the massively multiplayer online role-playing game Ragnarok as well as Kart Rider for about one year and she considered herself "addicted." As the interview went on, I found out that she and her boyfriend had been dating for a year and a half. It turned out that after the first six months of their relationship, she started playing computer games with him at PC bangs as a way to be together in a warm place during the winter. Being students, they did not have much money and it was the best solution for doing activities with one another on a budget. Although she said that the games she played were fun and the time she spent at PC bangs ranged from fifteen to twenty hours per week, throughout the interview it was clear that her motives for going to the PC bang were not so much about the games themselves, but rather what the venue offered for nurturing her relationship with her boyfriend. This was just one example that pointed me toward the myriad social reasons for spending a lot of time playing online games in Korea.

Yet another example from my interviews with gamers (Chee, 2006, p. 234) was of a couple in their early twenties, who met online by playing Lineage together almost forty hours per week. They credited their mutual passion for the game that initially allowed them to meet offline at a Lineage event. The man recalls seeing her and experiencing "love at first sight." The woman, however, did not notice him at first and ignored his advances at the meeting. Afterwards, they would encounter one another online in Lineage, and he would try to get noticed by stepping in to protect her from harm during enemy attacks. After a while, this impressed her enough so that she consented to finally going on a date with him. Their relationship slowly evolved. After a year and a half, the couple told me they were helping one another cut down on the time they spent online playing Lineage but were still going to PC bangs and using them as places they could meet.

In recent years, seeing my previous informants court, find careers, and get married has been interesting from a games point of view as well. Consoles have become more popular, and tend to be given as "housewarming" or marriage gifts as a symbolic gesture that the couple will game together once living together. I have been told that the infatuation with the console lasts about two weeks and then proceeds to "gather dust.'

## STARCRAFT AND THE RISE OF ONLINE GAME SPECTACLES: ESPORTS

StarCraft is a clear example of how form has trumped content. If one is discussing how online games came to occupy a place in Korean mainstream culture, it is essential to highlight the central role Blizzard's real-time strategy (RTS) game StarCraft played in the popularizing of online games in the Korean imagination. In North America, the StarCraft franchise enjoyed some popularity, but not nearly to the extent that it has in Korea. Considering that StarCraft is a game that was released in early 1998, it has been both remarkable and perplexing that such a game would continue being popular more than two decasde later—the twenty-fifth anniversary of its release coinciding with the publication of this book. It certainly captured the imagination of the government agency manager I interviewed, who told me that his familiarity with games dated back to arcade games thirty years prior to our conversations. However, while working for a government television station years ago, he came across eSports.

> *[eSports] provided me with a totally different perspective. Media broadcasting at that time was suffering from a lack of content. Suddenly, they had a new phenomenon. Games. It was really interesting and I wanted to be a part of it somehow.*

He then started playing online games such as the popular Korean MMORPG Lineage and StarCraft, along with a whole host of other games, which he credits for his current work in the games industry. His time in and with members of the games industry and working with the government served to broaden his perspective, as he was in the process of starting his own games business when we last spoke.

## GAMES AND SOCIAL STATUS

*You could annihilate your boojangnim [director's] base and they can't say anything. <laughs> And you can laugh about it.*

—Salaryman

Related to the discussion on Confucian social structures, games also serve the role as a leveler of social hierarchy. On many an occasion, I have gotten the sense that the "real" workplace interaction in Korea occurs outside of a typical nine to five workday. This is evident in the "salaryman" culture, where the daylight hours are spent executing tasks, and the night is spent nurturing one's social/career ties. Online games have become part of this ecology in Korea as one of the mediating activities between colleagues—superiors and inferiors alike.

In the quote starting this section, my informant is talking about the relatively high barrier to social interaction, or expressing oneself in everyday Korean life. As I have mentioned in my own encounters, almost everything is done by introduction and networks. In the case of online games, the "networked" access lowers barriers to entry, as it provides an opportunity to interact with new people, or those with a previously high power-distance relationship (Hofstede, 1997), such as that of a superior/subordinate.

*If you have a common reason to talk, it's much easier. StarCraft provided the window for that. Other than drinking . . . [Games are] a group activity. Culturally, they don't come up to you and go, "Hello . . ." They don't say this a lot. Your life is your life, and you don't mix.*

## DEMARCATIONS: WANG-TTA AND CHAE MYUN

On the opposite end of games serving as a hierarchy leveler in some cases, the online game also serves as a site of negotiation for offline status.

During my earlier fieldwork in Korea, I came across what I identified as the Korean social issue of Wang-tta, which includes the act of singling out one person in a group for the purpose of bullying and ostracization. It is a difficult term to translate into English from Korean. One can be said to either "make Wang-tta" or be the object of Wang-tta. The term is paradigmatically similar to (and some have said manifesting in concert with) the Japanese term for bullying, Ijime. In reference to Ijime situations, Dogakinai (1999) stated that in collectivist societies such as Japan, similarity is a source of comfort, whereas difference is disparaged and subject to much abuse from others. While there are concepts along similar lines in other cultures such as scapegoating, the issue of Wang-tta is not commonly known or written about outside of Korea (Chee, 2006). The concept of Wang-tta exists in opposition to the admiration for people who can game excessively (and as a result, game well). After all, as a player quipped, "To be really good at something in Korea, you have to be crazy about it, or else you can't do it." It therefore made sense that a key motivation to excel at digital games is to not be the "Wang-tta" and be a full participating member of one's peer group.

It is important to include what one of my informants stated verbatim about Wang-tta, because it illustrates the aspects of gaming, peer pressure, and time investment so very well:

*If one class has forty people, thirty-nine people playing a game together, but one person can't play the game. Thirty-nine people then hate him, and he wants to play together with them but he couldn't because he can't play that well. So, after time goes, this gap is increased. So everyone hates him. Everyone hates him.*

Indeed, a primary motivator to play games in Korea appears to be so that one may achieve social acceptance among peers. The PC bang, in this way, provides a crucial moment in that it is an arena of talent exhibition in games. That is, one might practice playing at home, in order to "perform" at the PC bang where his or her talents in a game would then be scrutinized and "peer-reviewed."

Refusal to partake in game play could subject one to isolation and ridicule, which would severely impact someone's "chae myun" or "ability to save face." The fear of being made a "Wang-tta" could indeed motivate many young people to take every opportunity to practice the games of their peer groups to become more skilled and less subject to such ridicule. Also, the experience of gaming itself is time invested in nurturing a social network, and the worst thing would be for one to feel somehow left behind in skill, or movement as a group. Thus, not being good at games would be tantamount to possessing a social deficit, and present immense social pressure to invest time and effort into being good at games.

Another way of thinking about Wang-tta is through Johan Huizinga's (1955) discussion of the way spoilsports are treated. "The player who trespasses against the rules or ignores them is a 'spoil-sport' . . . Therefore he must be cast out for he threatens the existence of the play-community" (1955, p. 11). Roger Caillois (1961, p. 7) has concurred with Huizinga in that, "the game is ruined by the nihilist who denounces the rules as absurd and conventional, who refuses to play because the game is meaningless." In the Korean context then, anyone who threatens the sanctity of the play community subjects themselves to being singled out as Wang-tta.

In my studies, there have been acceptable circumstances for a player retreating from the group due to external circumstances. Such circumstances often include a once-frequent game player being removed from one's peer group for an extended period of time, for example, while doing compulsory military service for two years or going abroad to learn English for a year or more. Once such a player returns back to the home community, there may be more generosity regarding one's life changes. One may feel compelled to offer a vague reason such as, "it's no longer fun" or "my priorities changed." This reasoning, in retrospect, could be interpreted as a way to "save face" and not have one's lack of gaming practice be perceived negatively.

An example of the abatement in pressure to game can be seen in the story of an extremely hardcore game player who recalled engaging in tournaments that went on as long as thirty-six hours. However, his playing habits changed when he went to the UK for English language courses. While abroad, he found himself cut off from most of his peer group as well as Korea's broadband infrastructure. When I asked him what his major reason for cutting back on gaming was, he quipped:

*During my stay in England, that was a big reason. Their Internet speed is much slower. Very slow. I couldn't play a game [online] for nearly one year. So that's why. After that, I lost my temper. I lost interest in playing games.*

After his return to Korea, he resumed playing with his friends, but at a much lower rate. At the time of our interview, he spent "only" six to seven hours per week playing games in order to focus more on graduating. When I asked what he ended up doing during his time in England instead of playing online games, he responded with a chuckle that he had just gotten into alternative forms of recreation, including "Drinking. Smoking."

The concept of the Wang-tta effect illustrates the often-implicit concern over a lack of ability to participate in online game activities in peer groups after an absence. It also seemed important to be able to participate well after investing a lot of practice time. In my encounters with Korean gamers, in interviews and focus groups, the ability to do something "extremely well," in the areas of school or games, is very much taken seriously and admired.

As for women, there are also most definitely gender differences in the way women as opposed to men are esteemed in their peer groups. On more than one occasion, whether it was after losing a StarCraft match or an off-the-cuff remark after an interview, I have asked if I could ever be considered "Wang-tta" or made fun of in the way described for men. A specific response that was particularly telling of the wide gulf between gamer worlds in terms of gender was, "Of course not. Girls are different because they don't have to be good at games."

The common stereotype, which was reflected by the young women with whom I spoke, seems to indicate that women or girls tend to like "simple" games such as KartRider or Tetris, though as a number of scholars have reflected upon in their work, the motivations for online engagement are not only varied, but go far beyond "cute" as Hjorth (2006) writes, and involving a multitude of complex constructs of gendered identity and agency (Consalvo & Paasonen, 2002). Despite online game play still being heavily skewed toward male gamers, the gender implications of gaming continue to be a source of fascination that I am considering in future analyses of gaming communities.

## MILITARY SERVICE

When I was pivoting from my Master's to Doctorate level work, I had an interesting discussion with a professor at MIT after presenting some of my initial results arising from my Korean fieldwork. Given what I had argued in the session, he asked me a pointed question: "So, are you saying that South Korea plays games because of North Korea?" I paused for a second, and replied, "Yes. I suppose one could say that." The phrasing of the question may have been intentionally leading, but there was a certain truth in that statement that has remained and it gave me a way to elaborate upon my arguments in terms of geopolitics to a greater extent. I have since conducted fieldwork on game culture in Finland, which showed me interesting linkages between game culture, government investment, and compulsory military service that is well-curated at the Finnish Museum of Games.

In the specific case of the Korean peninsula, its geopolitics from a number of disciplinary standpoints have been explored, namely the threat of the communist North upon the democracy of the South. "Within half a decade, the Korean War brought new social and political dislocation, which still profoundly affects the nation" (Bedeski, 1983, p. 20). However, an explicit link between that threat, compulsory military service, and participation in online gaming in Korea is an original articulation found in this work drawn from my interviews and observations over the course of my research on Korea.

Though I did not travel to Korea looking for a link between military service, online games, and the condition of youth, I could not help but become aware of an existence so radically different from my relative lack of military exposure on the Canadian West Coast. The impact of compulsory military service, tales of those formative experiences, and the clear articulation of brotherhood bonds that result from that service pervade my field data. By drawing attention to this aspect of military service into the discussion of online games and mainstream Korea, I hope to show how, like education, the focus on military activities is a confluence of culture, social structure, infrastructure, and policy, pointing very much to the values as they manifest in the Korean national context.

Through no urging on my part, my informants would bring up the two-year period of compulsory military service as a prominent aspect of a Korean male's coming of age. As one of my informants recounts:

*We stayed at the army base two years and two months. We could only go out forty-five days. That is the only vacation we have. Four or five times. Ten days. Ten days per vacation. During the army service, we cannot go out. Even though we go outside, we cannot do things like drink alcohol or play games.*

Clearly, there are issues such as these that present themselves in the social structures particular to Korean life. Among young Korean men, military service functions as both training and, more significantly in a social manner, a rite of passage that signals a clear demarcation between one's relatively carefree youth and responsible, career-oriented adulthood. The typical severing of social networks during this time of military service presents challenges for reintegration into civilian culture after isolation. Additionally, there are ambivalent feelings of the reception one will have, once back into the social network of origin.

When doing military service, the majority of recruits are cut off from Internet access and may only write letters to loved ones by conventional letter mail. Forty days off-site are permitted, and may be taken in increments of fewer than ten days. One may suppose that this temporary severance of civilian ties ensures that the social network becomes oriented around one's military cohort and that the conditions for forming a brotherhood bond become optimal.

As mentioned in the previous chapter regarding military policy, this compulsory service takes place in a Korean male's late teens or more generally, early twenties. Through what my informants told me, upon returning, it seemed as though there was a certain shock when re-entering the previous social network, and that spending time gaming with one's friends (at PC bangs, online, etc.) was a method of easing that re-entry. Less explicitly, one may socialize, meet people on online matchmaking sites, look for jobs, engage in e-commerce activities, and a whole host of other everyday activities enabled by broadband connectivity in Korea.

This compulsory military service could very well be thought of as in place "because of North Korea" and the complicated relationship with online gaming that results has occurred in ways previously unanticipated. Consequently, this aspect of Korean life has profoundly impacted the mechanics of youth culture in which hardly any aspect is left untouched, including the vast and overlapping communities to which one belongs. Moreover, that these factors are not typically in the same discussions as online games do much to speak to player motivations and life choices heading into middle-aged life: the condition of becoming a middle-aged man, an "Ajeossi."

During my 2004 sojourn, when I interviewed a twenty-five-year-old in his final year of university, he claimed he no longer played online games. Going on a hunch, I interviewed him anyway because I wanted to give him the space to have a dialogue with me about online gaming. It turned out that prior to his two and a half year break, he was, as he put it, "addicted to StarCraft." He played the game for four years seriously, and upon returning from military service, realized he was a "lower class player," and he quit "because I wasn't very good at StarCraft." Related to my initial hunch, and other observations that he spent time at PC bangs and had social gatherings focusing on game play, I probed further by asking if he went to PC bangs for his friends. His response was illuminating:

*Yes, mostly. I go to [the] PC room with my friends to play games with my friends. But if I go just by myself it's not fun. I'm not good at games, but if I go to a PC bang with my friends, we can make a team and play with other teams. So it's [a] kind of socialization. So I like that. Not playing by myself. Before we went to the army, we played StarCraft all the time together. When I was in the army, I was dying to go online. I wanted to play StarCraft, but I couldn't. They didn't allow it. After I quit the army, of course I played StarCraft, but it wasn't very much fun compared to before the army. I was defeated by people.*

Indeed, reflections such as his, along with my observations of those who have returned from military service, seem to speak to the feeling of being somewhat "adrift" socially. The remedy to that feeling of re-entry after isolation becomes using games as a medium of communication to facilitate the reinsertion of oneself into a social network, whether it be in the PC bangs, online, or offline. These have been some of the practices enabling the reconstitution and reconstruction of a sense of sociality and belonging in a civilian context.

## RETURNING TO PLAY AGAIN

This chapter discussed the role online game play has in the broader culture, social structure, and infrastructural environment of Korea. Rather than anti-social activity gaming portrayed in global media, the examples provided here show games as an extension of the self in order to reach out to others.

By understanding online games as a communication medium, we are then able to understand that it is a means of facilitating human connection, rather than cutting it off. Instead of Korea being a mysterious nation of game addicts, we are able to see that there have been a number of other factors that contribute to the popularity of online gaming among youth.

*Chapter 4*

# Gender Pipelines and Pipe Dreams

## *Games Industry and Mobility*

One chilly night in the middle of winter, after an evening of barbeque and norae bang with a group of friends, we squeezed ourselves into one of the many taxis prowling Seoul to get back to our respective homes. Joking amongst ourselves, and then including the taxi driver Ajeossi, we all felt a sense of camaraderie with one another. As we passed by an exit on the freeway that pointed toward the direction of Busan, (about 200 miles from Seoul) I made an off-hand joke that we should just keep going to Busan. The taxi driver's eyes grew wide and he immediately asked everyone in the car if they wanted to go to Busan. We all agreed that while it was an amusing notion to entertain, that we couldn't possibly take a taxi from the top end of the country to the other, even if it meant five hours of driving through the night.

The driver's tone got serious. "I'll drive you there for 150,000 Won." We laughed it off and talked about how crazy an idea that would be, while doing the math. He countered our banter with, "120,000 Won then. You can't beat that. It's winter. You're comfortable." We assured him that as tempting an offer as that was, we were only joking and we simply could not take off spontaneously. As we proceeded to chat about other things, the driver, seeing that the last exit for Busan on that stretch of freeway was imminent, slowed the car down and crept into the exit lane. He asked one last time, "Are you sure you don't want to go to Busan?" We insisted that we did not. Slightly deflated, he slowly returned to the main freeway, saying how nice the journey would have been. Upon reflection, the taxi driver's behavior was not without reason.

Recounting the events with the taxi driver to a friend the next day, they shrugged, and merely said, "Yeah. It's hard to earn 100,000 Won."

## ECONOMIC EVERYDAY PRESSURES

In Korean, it would not be uncommon to hear someone say, "It's very hard to earn 100,000 Won," whether it be for reasons of class entrenchment, debt in a globalizing society, or the precarious nature of jobs still felt at the street level in the days since the Asian Economic Crisis. Our taxi driver in the story above would have most definitely preferred ending up in Busan with a guaranteed lump sum for the night, more than his usual uncertainty-filled grind of 4,000–8,000 Won fares throughout the wee hours of the morning.

This chapter is a discussion of the games industry and the opportunities for upward mobility in Korea given the inflections of gendered forms (and norms) of labor in context. Bearing in mind the previous chapter's discussion of common youth gaming practices, yet another facet of the question concerning how gaming has become such a mainstay in the Korean economy becomes even more apparent in the sections to follow, outlining the challenges faced by the online games industry. This portion presents the issues that became apparent through my ethnographic fieldwork, further supported by in-depth interviews with government and industry insiders. The economic pressures, though less visible due to many instances of multigenerational living arrangements, have been highlighted as a major concern in mainstream Korean media. This concern is primarily due to the declining sense of meritocracy, as it used to be the case that education was a guarantee of upward socioeconomic mobility and success, whereas at present there is no such guarantee and a degree is merely the price of admission into a veritable gladiator's arena of competition. Many university graduates still cannot find jobs (Oh & Larson, 2011, p. 6). One example using the persuasive narrative of a bootstrapped individual having changed his stars from modest beginnings includes former President Roh Moo Hyun, who studied for the Korean bar exam without enrolling in law school. Such days are already viewed as somewhat of a golden age, as students with advanced degrees from prestigious universities are currently unable to find employment.

Due to the twenty-four-hour nature of cities like Seoul, there is almost always something open for business. This also meant that if I were walking around a plaza in the middle of the night, it would not be out of the question to wake a shopkeeper from a nap to make one's transaction. I often wondered if—and eventually made an educated guess that—this was probably not the shopkeeper's only occupation and that instead of isolated incidents, working around the clock had become a normal fact of life. In recent years, youth unemployment and the general precarious nature of work has become an increasing concern in Korea and the world over. As the critically acclaimed movie *Parasite* and popular Netflix sensation *Squid Game* have brought even more awareness of the prevalence of economic desperation (along with overt misogyny), there are more young women employed than men for predictable reasons of military service and the consequences resulting from that hiccup in one's education and socialization.

Most of the time, the work is precarious, part time or fixed term contracts. Even with university degrees, a small fraction of those graduates earn a "decent" income of $2,000 USD per month. Such conditions of employment have approximately one fifth of workers supplementing their incomes with second and third jobs, as the contribution from those jobs can range anywhere from an extra 10 to 50 percent per month over one's main source of income. With more precarity and ways to generate side incomes through social media and informal economies, many have thrown up their hands in attempts to make inferences on reported income.

An executive I interviewed from NHN (Next Human Network) Corporation relates the positive effect this had on the online games industry acquiring talent:

> *Coming back to the point of the young talent, [those who] graduated from the major or renowned universities like Seoul National University or KAIST, or Korea, Yonsei Universities—those young talented individuals have joined the Internet games industry. Particularly because those young talents typically go to . . . the bar exam, or government official exam, or to conglomerates. After that IMF crisis, the public sees that the engineers in those conglomerates had to leave the company. So, doctors, medical schools, became very popular. At the time, people wanted more stable jobs.*

Koreans have expressed dismay that the persistently grim job market that has resulted in typically high-prospect doctoral degree holders or those with prestigious degrees obtained overseas competing for unpaid internships, have only seemed to drive up competition for jobs in small and medium-sized enterprises. Despite the real need for creative and artistic work, prospects for humanities majors remain even grimmer. They have little hope in finding jobs in their areas due to decades of prioritization of training in STEM disciplines. It is this context that made the manifestation of a robust game culture and industry dynamics particularly intriguing to study and situate for the purposes of this study.

## CAREERS AS GAME-MAKERS AND PLAYERS

> *One of my colleagues mentioned, "Why do you keep playing those online games? What do you want to be when you grow up?" If you said "I want to work in a game company," your parents would go crazy. But actually,*

> our company, the parents want them to go to a conglomerate. Social . . . they're showing, the young generation, ah you must have company working like Google. Former generation said, earn enough money.
>
> —Michael

While, at present, careers in the Korean games industry are generally well regarded, the reasons for those jobs maintaining their status as viable options for success remain unclear.

Curious about these factors, I incorporated a longitudinal aspect to my Korean fieldwork. That is, I was able to keep up with the trajectory of some key informants from my first study, who had self-identified as current or recovering games addicts. In my visits years later, they had since started careers in the games industry in roles ranging from developers to managers, to executive and directorial roles. Their thoughts regarding the industry from a domestic and globalizing point of view are presented below. Several of these informants had occupied, then quit or rejected higher paying prestigious careers with major chaebols like LG or Samsung in order to obtain a sense of greater fulfillment and operate outside the typical confines of hierarchy, as they saw it.

Michael, an executive for a major games portal, mused about potential reasons including the lack of formality and mobility:

> S: It was like Google at the time [of the venture boom season 1998–2000]. You didn't have to wear a suit and tie. Brilliant ideas needed . . . at that time people still wanted conglomerates but young talent ventured into these venture companies.
>
> F: They could make something of themselves early in life.
>
> S: Right.

The lack of formality also extended to the semi-corporeality of corporations. Michael mused aloud at how large companies could operate out of "parking garages," which was an indicator of this moment of transition from brick and mortar firms to more distributed models:

> They create games software, then they upload it for free. They become Nexon. After NCSoft IPO, Mu—success. Venture capital started investing in games industry and some talented guys were flown in. Design, game design, graphics, after that they were able to organize companies into online game companies.

Mina, a game producer I interviewed with whom I formed a rapport through numerous Korean online games events, suggested that the lack of other accessible forms of entertainment for youth was due to a history of censorship as mentioned earlier with reference to the Public Performance Act.

*Could be partly my personal experience being a part of production, but when I look at Korea, there isn't much entertainment that young people can enjoy. The music industry is very limited and small, and we used to have a law that bans a certain type of music performance before we became a full democracy. So if that's the case what do the children do? They play computer games and on top of playing games they want to make them. I think it was a part of lack of entertainment and we don't have much of a playground or nature to play so they're stuck in their house and they start making games.*

## RECRUITMENT

I caught up with one of my informants from the early days of the 2004 study who, at that time, was a self-professed recovering game addict. Gene subsequently became involved in the games industry as an engineer turned developer, and has provided an excellent longitudinal example of someone who was in the throes of intense game play who then went on to have a career in the local games industry. Gene provided his input regarding the process of recruitment, through his years of experience in the industry. He explained:

*They recruit from Internet sites like Daum Korea or they post the recruit[ment notice] under their homepage. The gaming culture is very well acknowledged by the students so they voluntarily find the recruiting. The major game company also [recruits] the same way like Samsung . . . once or twice a year.*

On the other hand, an executive in the games industry, Michael, provided a more network-oriented viewpoint to recruitment. His input tempered Gene's relative optimism, given that it implied the persistence and importance of old elite school networks.

*S: At that time, those young talents who studied management, majored in engineering science, they joined Naver, Daum. The Hangame community [was] also from Yonsei University, Nexon also—all at the school [where] they all knew each other, that kind of thing. They were like conglomerates.*

*F: Were they from outside Korea?*

*S: Inside. At the initial stage they were mostly from inside. Before, Korean films were only something for the old people. So only Hollywood movies were worth going to big cinema. At that time, Korean movies had popularity over Hollywood movies because they had Korean humor. That's something that foreign movies could never get. Those born after 1970, they were the new generation.*

S: Still, students study in other majors because the professors and instructors aren't trained in that, you know? Or computer engineering or animation, or cartoon and the others are not from games industry. Not many people from the successful developers, they didn't turn in their careers to professor.

F: So how would a person get a job in the games industry then if not by schooling then by what?

S: These days, the marketing or business development, the big companies they recruit from the universities. NCSoft, they hire from SNU, Yonsei Universities, they do well.

## BETWEEN THE LOCAL AND THE GLOBAL

> You know so we invest a lot of money, and the Korean games get made for less than 3 million dollars and they don't do very well outside of Korea but it's a very hard mindset. I mean, you look at Blizzard spending 60 million some of the American cycles are 25–30 million we're 10 percent of their development costs. Pretty easy to do. But here, there's enough and all these work, so they think why would we spend another half million . . .
>
> —Joel

At games industry events in Korea, I would often engage with personnel from business development, sales, and development representing local and global games companies. These immersive experiences were excellent opportunities to learn about the priorities of different groups in this industry through a range of formal and informal ways. From the first "business-matching" events in which I sometimes participated as a volunteer liaison, I became keenly aware of Korea's saturation of local development talent that was in desperate need for international partners, mostly in the form of investment, and publishing/distribution. On the one hand, the local struggle was how to get Korean games published globally due to a glut of games development talent. On the other hand, the global to local challenge involved employing local talent in the effort to localize popular games like World of Warcraft in terms of language, play, and content.

> Joel: Korean companies—they used to do everything in house, and now that's changing. Even big companies like NCSoft, they started buying solutions from outside vendors. So I guess by giving up some part they created a market for industry technology of companies.

There is also the concern from everyone about Chinese competition. "Already . . . Chinese custom online games are more competitive than Korean online games." Michael noted that without localization efforts, "we will lose everything ... this cultural thing, we should favor our local. So it's more than protectionism. Korean games are losing ground." In essence, it makes sense that geopolitical concerns are influencing how games are made, played, localized, and popularized in Korea.

## A FLATTER HIERARCHY IN GAMES CAREERS

When I asked Gene about the attraction to these jobs in the local Korean games industry, he emphasized that the opportunity for creativity came from small team sizes and a less pronounced hierarchy as a game developer, rather than what he might find working for a large company.

> *Yeah of course it's creative but overall, the big companies ... are getting their projects ready. The thing is there aren't that many people in the team so the difference between the manager and the team manager and director is not so hierarchical.*

Related to the discussion of games being relatively new and small-scale enough to subvert traditional viewpoints regarding Confucian age-based hierarchies, this "flatness" appeared to be a major attraction to my informants. The relative openness with one's superiors in dialogue and trading ideas is an attractive aspect of a career in Korea that leaves many who work for the larger chaebols wanting:

> *We can really bring up the ideas or we can do the work really, and not be criticized for joining, gathering. And also we don't need to do full-time work without any things to do. And also we have a better chance to go up.*

What Gene was emphasizing here was that the typical corporate culture was not as dynamic as newer gaming companies, nor were elites as entrenched in the gaming companies as their equivalents in the chaebols, so that there was more room for growth. Moreover, the founders of the most successful games companies had up to five years of experience in major chaebols. For example, NCSoft was primarily founded by those with experience at Hyundai.

> *Right. But they found it not suitable for them. They had some feeling of limit to what they could do, but they were able to venture into other things because it was new. Having their own business was of course a salaryman's dream. But of course [in] the early days it was unconventional [by] Korean ... standards. [It] was possible because they were more experienced.*

The flatter hierarchy was further realized due to the generational gap in expertise with Internet technologies and the broader information economy. While some would see the intergenerational gap in technological literacy as a hindrance, Michael outlined the positive aspects for those less senior and entrenched in the established power structures:

> They cannot compete against the elderly people established in their early forties, fifties. [The elders] had the knowledge, connections but, like the Internet, "What? What's that? What for?" [The younger people] were the only guys who know about programming, computers, and computer entertainment. [The elderly] don't have the experience [figuring out] what the Internet, the computer, can do. They were kind of like—walls—the entry barrier for them.

He credits the introduction of "HiTel" by Korea Telecom in 1991, which was similar to the AOL service in the United States of "You've Got Mail" fame. Computers were something that the older generations feared or even abhorred.

> Their advance, in a way, before in their generation, the experienced ones had the authority in the long period. Now those who are in an entry level can compete. But our generation was exposed to computers and HiTel, they were not afraid of computers, the Internet and tools, web. They were able to go out to the world.

Moreover, the freedom inherent in smaller, more level hierarchies found in the information industries has been more attractive than the prospect of working in a larger company as told by Mina:

> F: So, what makes you stick with independent consulting as opposed to going to work for a major company?
>
> S: Freedom. And, well, I've worked in a company before and the organizational setting is fun, but starting from scratch to set up something that I was in is also fun as well. Whatever I see, if I come up with an idea I can just stick out my business card and make it a business. That's freedom. Complete freedom.

## INDUSTRY HISTORY ACCORDING TO THE INDUSTRY

In the earlier part of this book, I laid out the sociohistorical factors of what I believe to be the catalytic forces behind what has helped the games industry in Korea be as successful as it is. This section presents the perspectives of those in the games industry and their own impressions of what has occurred, and challenges along the way.

I interviewed Joel, who represented the global perspective of an international company that was working with the local Korean games industry in order to develop global markets for their products. Given that he had been based in Asia and visiting Korea for over ten years, I asked him his opinions regarding what has brought the Korean games industry to its current state. He identified four primary things:

1. A captive cultural market.
2. A "tendency toward piracy, which meant that the cultural market wouldn't thrive anyway."
3. Platform and the PC bang culture.
4. Key movers and shakers in the right time/place: "I think the Korean guys, the Korean industry was very very bright, the guy from Nexon, NCSoft, were clearly innovators at the right time and the right place."

Regarding the captive cultural market, Joel was referring to the idiosyncratic nature of the Korean technoscape—linguistically with its use of Hangeul as well as sociocultural tastes that have been difficult for global firms to address, let alone penetrate. The second element, a tendency toward piracy, was dismissive in tone due to the prevailing notion and practice of what the West would typically classify as piracy. His third point, of PCs as the gaming platform of choice, lumped in with the role played by the PC bang is consistent with my assertions (Jin & Chee, 2008) that the PC platform and the PC bang is an important modality to consider. As Japanese consoles were not significant in Korea during the economic crisis, "PCs [were] the gaming platform of choice in Korea [during] the economic downturn . . . when a bunch of guys got up in the morning and had nothing to do except go and sit in a PC bang, and they didn't want to say to their wives that they had lost their jobs." Additionally, and related to the PC bang culture, he stated that, "I don't think there are as many entertainment choices for the average Korean as there is for the average American." Lastly, along with the perfect storm of events that contributed to the present game culture that I wrote about in documenting the rise of gaming in Korea, he mentions that, "The Korean government also wanted to make Korea the digital capital of the world. The agencies had a real profound effect on the digital games industry, like KGDI." In the following section, I will discuss how the industry makes sense of the perfect storm of events.

## THE IMF CRISIS AND OPPORTUNITY

There was a great deal of maneuvering in the game industry around the time of the IMF crisis. Of course, these are but a subsection of success stories of making lemonade from lemons. However, in this respect my informants including Joel, Michael, and Mina, who recounted stories of economic collapse, coping strategies, and subsequent success, were ideal.

According to Michael, during the IMF crisis during 1998, there was a concurrent Internet boom with numerous outfits calling themselves "dot-com," "and you find investors, and that's it." That was the status quo until approximately the year 2000. Meanwhile, a number of talented younger individuals, having benefited from investment in the knowledge industries, were starting to flood the marketplace with their talent. "[During] the venture boom season [of] 1998–2000, most of the companies, called Web Agencies, made home pages for corporations. At the time, [the] government advertised that we had to be number one in [the] information revolution. Otherwise, we, Korea, would lag." With that last statement regarding Korea, he looked off into the distance, and what followed connects to earlier comments on Korean-Japanese relations and technology:

*Because we once had that experience one hundred years ago. Which was 1910, and we ended up colonized by Japan. Because at that time when the Western countries came and opened the market for trade, that's when Korea closed the door. Father of King Gojong. The government reminded us that a century ago, we failed because we closed our country. Now we have to go forward and we should be the pioneers.*

The use of nationalism and the specter of failure against foreign powers are repeatedly invoked in efforts to mobilize the nation and galvanize sentiment. In this case, it was used to sell the Information Society to the Korean public. The use of keywords, slogans, and propaganda was readily apparent in popular media.

*S: This is once in a century experience. That's why Hana Telecom was able to do that, because otherwise it must have been very hard. Of course it was an investment business, but Korean Government [was] interested, so [they] pretended not to see so they [did] not intervene.*

*F: Ah, so backstage.*

*S: Yeah, backstage approval. But in the message advertising that information is the key. Basically we should be first to make something. IT was the key word for government. IT, venture, globalization, "Americans: stand back."*

The last statement of "Americans: stand back," was referring to the external audits and admonishment the chaebols received during the crisis period, when many of the conglomerates were forced to liquidate their assets. Whether it was the specter of Japanese colonization or the deftly constructed proto specter of American neocolonialism, the call to action resulted in effective marketing for the Korean information industries.

> S: *After the success of the movie industry, the government actually . . . had a cultural budget and they distributed it to some of the VCs. Venture was the key word. Popular. Venture was the only way for Korea to move forward. They needed political slogans, and stuff like that. Anyway, at that time, that's what made PCs. Some portion of money to the gaming industry.*

## A LEGITIMATE AND RESPECTABLE INDUSTRY

With the direct infusion of cash along with relatively minimal restrictions, online games soon became a legitimate and respectable line of work in which to be involved. Mina notes that games have transformed from being thought of as the province of child's play to being recognized as a business "with authority" and multimillion dollar transactions. While at first blush it may seem a matter of trivial categorization and semantics, it was the very matter of classification that could either hinder or help the viability of online games companies at crucial points. Michael draws attention to how the listing of a company affects the rates at which games could borrow money. "NHN used to be number one in capital at ten trillion Won. After this financial crisis, it went down. In Korea there are two stock markets. Korea Stock Exchange and . . . it moved from KOSDAQ. It was quite inconvenient [to games people]. When you go to the bank and borrow loan you get a better rate to those who work in a listed company. When your company is listed in KOSPI, big bank, then you get a better rate." Where analysts previously covered the industries as consolidated entities, the Internet industry was disaggregated from divisions such as semiconductors.

> S: *Samsung electronic, cover Naver let's say, NCSoft at the same time. Now it's more specialized and separate. The one analyst that specializes in entertainment, and one analyst covers all those players. Internet, games, and also gambling.*

So, on the one hand the figures are more auditable, but confusing in a different way, as Internet, games, and gambling are still under the same classifications. "Covered sometimes at the same time, but still, it's still game or online game and portal are still in the same group." This realization of qualitative differences within quantitative classifications presents many implications including that of policy, but despite that, lent the large numbers needed to launch the online games industry into a widely recognized industry with financial clout.

# MILITARY SERVICE AND THE INDUSTRY— SAME SAME, BUT DIFFERENT

> *[For] the Korean male, the military is an issue. Two to three years in the military in their critical time [of life] is a big issue.*
>
> —Michael

As earlier chapters have shown, the military is an inextricable part of life on the Korean peninsula. This section opens up the issue of military service specifically in terms of its dynamic with the Korean IT workforce from the perspective of those involved with the games industry. Though I did not have explicit questions regarding military service in my interview guide, my informants would broach the topic of their own accord. Their perspectives were always slightly different from one another, and immensely fascinating. It showed me how very much military service was a fact of living life in Korea, and as someone who was studying an industry dominated by men already steeped in a patriarchal culture, it made sense to embrace a study of this important phenomenon as it pertains to how people make sense of their social roles.

Research by Royse, Lee, Undrahbuyan, Hopson, and Consalvo (2007), systematically analyzed the challenges involved with women and games, articulating the numerous assumptions, viewpoints, and types of engagement involved in this area of scholarship. As my earlier research allowed for my engagement with subjects to occur without deliberately recruiting women, the analysis unsurprisingly focused on the challenges facing mostly young men in these gaming spaces as the de facto majority. Though I did not have the bandwidth to engage with the gender dynamics and very real resentments increasingly abound around and through the industry, my research in the last decade has been able to take these issues on with a larger community of scholars and practitioners through explicitly feminist and ethical subject lenses as in Amanda Cotes's *Gaming Sexism* (2021), or the nuanced treatment of race in Tara Fickles's *The Race Card* (2020).

Michael's input regarding the contingency of IT work during an otherwise rather definite period of a Korean male's life is important to focus attention upon here, because military service is often discussed as a matter of course.

> *And the Korean government said, was . . . if pass an exam and prove you are able, instead of going to the military you can work in an IT company, because young companies have a hard time finding good talent. They don't know when they will go bankrupt.*

What Michael describes is a type of "alternative" military service, which allows those trained in STEM related disciplines to spend three to five years in an IT company instead of going through conventional military training. While not all of these recruits went to Internet or online game related companies, one can imagine how this alternative stream might be attractive to youth. The classification of the companies also mattered differently years ago: "IT had such a broad meaning at that time. But still the thing is IT/Internet are different but still at that time they were categorized as a pack."

Naturally, upon realizing what Michael was saying to me, a disconcerting feeling settled over me, considering how until then, I had talked to people who had extolled the virtues of going for military service and presented it as a matter of course. I asked him just how big the numbers were, to which he responded, "Mmm . . . not that big because they have to pay—I mean they have to pass. It depends on the university." He explained that there are the divisions between the Arts and Sciences, Mungwa and Igwa, respectively. Those who go toward Mungwa are not eligible for exemption of this nature and the design of the system was quite confusing at the onset, with some in gray zones joining the IT industries.

> 1990s to the end of 2000, the literature [students] take advantage [and went toward the] technology service degree [requirements] and so of course they do Business. Those young talents were able to go to Naver, NCSoft, and the programmers, but sometimes those Mungwa, they thought they [were] programmer(s) but in reality they work in the business side, the social. But anyway my point is they join the Internet and game industries.

Thoroughly intrigued by this potential motivation to join the IT industries, I mused that the Korean males with whom I had discussed military service were extremely proud of the fact that they had gone through those years, and that they talk about how close they are to their "brothers." I mentioned that it was quite unusual to not go for military service, at which point Michael's tone seemed more hushed, and he acknowledged this in the affirmative. "Military is something like a hot potato, especially for Social Services, and public office stuff. It is something that you should do." He proceeded to tell me that though the public sentiment is that everyone must and therefore should go for military service, if it is at all possible to be exempted, people would undoubtedly jump at the chance.

> F: Doesn't it affect the rest of your career if you do not?
>
> S: At that time, yah, but Presidential Candidate Lee—when he compete[d] against Dae Jung Kim, actually Lee lost, mainly, he lost because his son was

*[exempted]. Military. From that perspective, of course to go for public office, you have to [do the service].*

He conceded that it was necessary to maintain that the majority of people had to go for military service, or the whole system would be compromised.

*F: Do you think it makes the IT field more attractive to young men, or is it not a factor?*

*S: It's a sensitive subject. If I knew that then, I would also want to join. But at that time . . .*

*F: Why doesn't everyone want to do this then to escape military service?*

*S: There's not much room for that I think . . . But you know, [those at a] low level, they don't get it. Because otherwise, parents would never [allow their children to] go . . . bribing, paying, everything to get their sons exempted so it [would be] worth it. People [are] definitely upset, "Oh you're exempted from military service? Then you are the son of God." And there is a . . . minimum type of service: "Oh you are the son of a human." Regular military service? "Oh you are the son of darkness . . . <chuckles>"*

*F: <laugh>*

*S: [I] Very jokingly say [this], but it kind of reflects the society.*

It would be reasonable to believe that the incentives to join the IT industry might have served to direct talent toward those areas than they might have otherwise.

*F: If someone joins the IT industry, and then doesn't go for military service, do they have to stay in IT?*

*S: No no. It's only two to three years, not over five years. Of course [the company can make] a very competitive offer and they do thing[s] like get a degree. Many of them actually stay, and they help the young company to grow. Some of them get reward for that but it's their choice.*

Michael credited this government policy with allowing young talent to populate mid-sized companies in Korea, which have been typically short of skilled knowledge labor. The older generations in the chaebols could not fulfill this role, and this was the opportunity for early career mobility in the Korean IT industries.

## ONLINE SPENDING AND EARNING

*If you think of it like a hobby, like fishing, you can buy really expensive things. It's the same.*

—Gene

As one may see, online games in Korea have meant more than play and leisure. The nurturing of this industry has presented youth with opportunities to generate their own income at earlier ages, and navigate the challenges present in a post-IMF crisis economy. Having its own idiosyncrasies, the Korean market has demanded different strategies for users and companies alike in terms of local economic challenges and business models. Through sustained conversations with industry leaders and observations of the mechanics at the user level, I was able to catalog some of the primary differences between models that may have worked in North America but do not in Korea, and vice versa. Michael talked about the early days of microtransactions:

*We tried the item sales model, and that was quite successful. 10 cent, small amount of money or something like that—users are willing to pay. So with Lineage success, users are exposed to the idea that you can play game and you can pay for Internet entertainment.*

One example is the shift from subscription-based games to free-to play, the nature of which is notably described in Christopher Paul's 2020 book, *Free to Play*. In my discussion with Gene, who manages localization efforts of games from all over the globe for the Korean market, he asserted that the differences in game markets were both cultural and technical. For many Korean users, the American model of a subscription-based game was simply too high a barrier for entry, economically or psychologically.

One may observe this to be the case in other emergent economies where, for reasons of piracy or financial constraints, the North American business models do not work. Therefore, the microtransaction business model, where a user plays the game for free but can buy in-game items, has been much more successful. As online gaming is a largely social endeavor, more users at the onset of a game begets more users. Staying in the game, one is more inclined to make purchases for status, vanity, or other reasons. Subscription models have typically failed in Korea due to the competitiveness of the market.

*S: Many MMORPGs [have] already turned to micropayments. The only subscription model in Korea is Lineage I and II and World of Warcraft. Only three games are subscription based. Most games accepted micropayments. In Asian countries, they accept. The remaining markets are European and North*

*American. I think they're still worrying about the web-hosting fee. Basically when the game is created they have to pay more for hosting the game servers.*

Since the time of the interview, even World of Warcraft has gone free-to-play in order to keep up with the rapid dominance of gaming on social network sites and other low-barrier to entry games as written about extensively in Chess (2017).

Another example is what some may derisively call the "pay-to-win" model, where players with enough incentive to win over others are willing to use money to gain in-game advantage.

*S: If people want to have strong character, they pay for character and building up. You already know that. Money for one level, and they're making their own business, and they gather, like eight players. So two: they can get items. Their business is getting items and making money from characters leveling up, so they can get really unique item[s] really unable to compare to other[s]. Lineage is a competitive game and if you are strong you can really conquer everyone.*

Players can typically acquire goods on auction sites such as Itembay, but now more so by "network." "Game items that can sell for cash in the Korean market is valuable, so the game companies work to make it sellable." Prior to joining the games industry, Gene had many years of experience making money from selling in-game items as he was going through university.

When I asked Michael about why he thought Koreans would be willing to make microtransactions for their gameplay, and he noted a number of things, including gambling appeal:

*The game can contain kind of a gambling thing. Of course it was a potential legal issue, so they were very careful, but they sell game money. It could be like, under avatar, with that model, everybody. If you apply to Hangame, you create your own avatar, you can buy clothes.*

The PC bang also had a role to play in minimizing the practicality of subscriptions in the Korean context.

*Of course with Lineage you have a monthly subscription, but you pay $25 for the game, and you pay $2 for per hour use at [an] Internet café. At that time [that] made a lot of users, and showed them what they can do. Try it at an Internet café, and they think ok let's try, and then they think they want to have that environment in their house.*

An instructive moment was during an outing with one of my friends at a PC bang. Working for a games company every day, he had let his personal game account subscription lapse. However, when he logged on at the PC bang, he was still able to recover and resume his play through membership. Continuing on, the monetization models have evolved to more microtransactions and free-to-play modes, along with agile adaptive models that design gameplay in real time through automated processes.

## WOMEN IN THE GAMES INDUSTRY: A SHORT STORY

*"You don't look like a gamer."*

—Random Ajeossi

*"Why? What does a gamer look like?"*

—Me

While faring better in the games industry than in other more entrenched occupations, women are still nowhere near parity in what is often an environment that could be perceived as merely tolerant at its best and—as we see in current attitudes toward women in games—hostile and threatening at worst (Funk, 2012; Travers, 2000). The concerns highlighted in this section regarding women's mobility in the games industry encompass but a mere sample of challenges in career mobility that is important to consider because it presents yet another facet of how the online games industry may attract and retain talent. As in the case with North America, women are not typically streamed into gaming, as they are not into STEM disciplines. The same systematic barriers to participation exist in the Korean context. What I am showing here are possible motivations to play based on the opportunities one may find in a relatively new industry.

## THE ENEMIES OF GAMES

*I didn't add any negative, but online game, since it became more popular: the female group—we jokingly call the enemy of the Korean game industry.*

—Michael

During what I thought was the end of my interview with Michael, he made the above comment that I ended up pouncing upon, and probing further into, as it illustrates, with Korean ideological frames, the adversarial role into which women are typically cast when having anything to do with games. This pervasive ideology and rhetoric presents some immense challenges, which is consistent with my own more recent experiences and reports of online harassment and gender-based violence in Korea. When explicitly referred to as the "enemy" of the Korean games industry, I had to ask for clarification, and he proceeded to elaborate:

> *Parents, that means "Mom"—they always say they prohibit children from playing games. Online games, or whatever. Another is "Wife," they want their husband's time. They want their husband not to play online games. Instead of [gaming] she wants him to spend time with her.*

Typically female occupations were also implicated:

> *And, teachers. Most of the teachers now in Korea are female—no online games. Online games are thought to be the #1 factor that lowers the academic performance of children and mind stability.*

In this way, significant others like wives and girlfriends are not thought of as participants, but adversaries, and killers of all kinds of male forms of amusement.

> *Yes. Korean online game industry now faces some adversaries . . . it's like violent, or sexual issues of movies, novels, that kind of thing. Online games are regarded as some equal form of entertainment as sports. Hockey, soccer, basketball, or baseball. But it is not bad to play.*

Phrased in terms of an ultimatum and the "best of evils," gaming provides a way for males to indeed be technically and physically present in the household, while socializing and connecting with others in the Alone Together (Turkle, 2011) sense.

> *Of course girlfriends or wives want their husbands to spend more time with them instead of watching or playing sports, but which do you prefer? My playing online games or watching soccer?*

Indeed, one may see how this scenario of games serving a panacea for the otherwise painful nagging of females in the extra-domestic amusement endeavors of males can be just as harmful in the construction of female roles vis a vis a keystone industry like games.

In contrast, during the course of my fieldwork I had the chance to have sustained contact with Mina, who I had discussed earlier in the book given the experiences she shared with me. I found her to be a particularly dynamic woman in the games industry, and she recounted her experiences in navigating male-dominated Korean business culture. At the time of our formal interview, her activities centered on business development and sales around the gaming industry. Talking mostly to "Ajeossis," her days revolve around liaising with developers, engineers, purchasing departments, and relevant decision-makers.

The most interesting part of our interview was when the conversation meandered past my prepared questions. Because she was such an exceptional case in the games industry, I found her strategies in navigating the restrictions inherent in merely possessing a female body fascinating in gaining access to "the boys' club." One such example is the after-work hours networking activities that are crucial to career success in corporate Korea. The practices that involve consumption of alcohol and patronizing "room salons" into the wee hours of the night have served to alienate or keep the few women in the industry out of potentially beneficial career-oriented networking that often takes place at such gatherings. I wondered, though, about Mina's specific strategies for advancing her career and "playing along" with others who may be inclined to initially exclude her from activities.

> S: Well I like partying, so customers often feel uncomfortable because there is a woman's presence, but after they got used to it. So I think it's more a matter of a limit on the corporate card than my presence. There are some places that I'm not supposed to go, like a room salon.
>
> F: Do you go anyway?
>
> S: Ye-ye. Yeah. And then . . . well if it's my very close contacts, they don't care. They are like I look like a girl too. Sometimes yes, sometimes no . . .

Mina then described what she did for contacts with whom she had less of a rapport and who would be unsettled by her presence.

> Not so close contacts, take them [for] the first round. After they get a little tipsy and rowdy I just leave the [credit] card at the front and pay, and pick up the card the next day.

In terms of evening out, in the more recent years of discussion with Korean men in the game industry, they tell me that there are fewer expectations of after-work activities, citing more equitable acknowledgment of family responsibilities and professional behavior. Even more recently, men have been overtly incentivized to become parents and take a more active role in raising children due to Korea's record-setting decline in birth rate as of 2021. Dismissing activities like going to hostess bars as archaic, the ones who have made the switch from larger chaebols find the change refreshing in that most of the time, the everyday developer or company worker in smaller games companies do not have to partake as enthusiastically in these extreme corporate culture practices. The younger men see increased time away from the demands of work contexts as a benefit as well. Mina made note of this aspect, "The gaming industry I don't think they do room salon," but qualified it by saying that at times they inevitably blend together, "Korean business in general, especially Ajeossis in penguin suits they like room salons."

In general, the gaming industry is still touted as a much more relaxed environment for almost anyone feeling the constraints of rigid hierarchies and establishmentarianism. After all, according to Mina, those in the gaming industry tend to favor casual (as opposed to formalized) drinking, or going home and playing . . . games. "Let them do what they want to do. That is the best gift."

While working for men in subordinate positions, Mina noted that she was praised for achievements and treated well. However, when it came down to actually negotiating, she pointed to times where proceeding as a normal person proved too much of a mental barrier for the people with whom she was dealing.

> *That's a tough one. Gaming is a male dominant industry. But being a woman, the big problem is when I started seeing Ajeossis as an equal dealer. When you go face to face with the same weight of the deal—this is what I'm going to give you, so you give me this—I want this. I don't know why. On the negotiation table, they're not used to it. Not comfortable with it.*

Indeed, her being a female was at times so insurmountable a barrier that explicit requests for males were made.

> *Some people might directly tell you, "I much prefer male salesperson. Change the account manager." I was in that position before.*

Ultimately, Mina feels that the games industry provides a more relaxed and friendly environment that is relatively free of the very formal social meetings of corporate culture. "Even the Christmas card is formal. But the games [industry]: I don't have to be super friendly, and I can be natural and myself." So, in the meantime, she is staying put in the games industry.

## ATTRACTION AND REPULSION

Though the games industry has more opportunities for career mobility of younger people, traditional structural restrictions and biases are still very much apparent to this day. This chapter presented the everyday appeal of the games industry and how it manifested as an upwardly mobile career choice for many Koreans.

In speaking with those involved with the games industry and experiencing the enablers and constraints for myself, I identified how the industry was able to attract talent through a number of economic and political incentives afforded to those in the IT industries. Meanwhile, the reverberations from the upheaval of the IMF Crisis and the imperatives of military service for young Korean males continue to be felt in this industry, but in many ways discussed, these very contingencies were instrumental in propelling the Korean online games industry to its current level of prominence, legitimacy, and respectability. Online games are well-integrated into the Korean media ecology, and one may see this in terms of how online spending and earning in games, while having entirely different models from North American context, fit into the circumstances of Korean gameplay while attracting a number of people who are gaming for numerous and varied reasons.

The motivations one may have to join the online games industry are just as varied, but much has to do with the policy and culture. Flatter hierarchies in newer, less established companies that include younger talent, as well as a less entrenched corporate culture tend to be major attractions. Even those typically on the margins, such as women, who are constructed in adversarial terms have managed to find roles affording themselves more agency and decision-making in the games industry than in other career paths.

During my time in Korea, it became clear to me that activities like smoking were male activities (cigarettes were passed around freely in the military), but that women should not smoke. A woman smoking in public places was unseemly behavior, though I would see built-in ashtrays in women's washrooms everywhere, including universities where men smoked at their office desks. This indicated that there was an awareness of such activities occurring, but that they should not take place in public. I asked Mina about her perceptions regarding these taboo activities:

*F: Do you think it would be any different if you were a foreign looking woman?*

*S: Yes. Because Korean people have a dual standard. For example . . . a foreign woman smoking a cigarette, if she's good looking, people would say, "Wow, she looks so cool. Just like a movie star." If she's an ugly foreign looking woman smoking, people would say, "Oh. She's a foreigner." Nobody cares. And if it's a Korean woman who smokes . . . older generations would say—she's a bad girl.*

Being a smoker herself, it was not surprising that Mina explicitly brought up smoking as a sore spot.

> *Young people, a lot of guys my age say they don't care, but not for their girlfriends; not for their future wives. That's just one example of how Korean people would view foreign women and Korean women.*

As I have hinted, one notable exception has been the PC bang for acting as a gray zone for public/private behavior outside the gaze of those who might scrutinize youth behavior. Women freely lit cigarettes at PC bangs, and it is completely unremarkable behavior in that context. Perhaps they would be inclined to find a game to play during that time.

Clearly, there is a long way to go, but there are many appealing aspects of online games to young Koreans. Accordingly, there are many reasons for a thriving games industry that have very little to do with games. This initiative has been lauded for allowing young talent to populate mid-sized companies in Korea, which have been typically short of skilled knowledge labor. As older generations employed in the large chaebol companies could not typically fulfill these roles, this was a major opportunity for early career mobility in the Korean IT industries that would not have existed for youth otherwise.

If the military service requirement is fulfilled by men working at a games company for three to five years, which then results in networking opportunities and skill building for those men, it means that typically women are systemically shut out of this specific process entirely despite their possible training precisely because of their gender. Women would then enter into the game industry later, if ever, or participate in the industry by other means and specializations. As a result, the prevailing notion that women do not become game developers because they are not interested in STEM and/or games is entirely oversimplistic. Even if, hypothetically, girls were not socialized away from STEM and games as they are in other countries like the United States, they have been and are still in this case turned away from opportunities for participation in a growing proportion of the Korean information economy at the crucial junctures of educational, friendship, and business networks at their nascent and founding stages. Given that the reasons for gaming and getting into the games industry to begin with are so very divided along gender lines already, in the Korean context these policies serve to reinforce existing gender norms beyond that of just the military. Rather, the perspective for which I have advocated is that games do not exist in a vacuum. Instead, the current online game culture includes a number of inextricable dependencies in a national media ecology.

*Chapter 5*

# Gaming the Future

## *Holding Space for Better Worlds*

When I first started researching online game addiction in 2002, I knew very little about Korea and had only the most passing familiarity with its history and people. Two decades later, things have certainly changed, and my time there, through research and friendship, has been utterly transformative for the way I regard games and culture. It has both informed, and laid the foundation for my approach to examining contextual issues in technology and society, namely seeing online games as a medium of communication. My subsequent interest in Korea's gamers, language, and culture developed very much as an anthropological thirst for participating in and observing the everyday lived realities of an intriguing set of people. Though examining the role of online games in Korean life may have served as the initial spark of interest, it lit a fire that illuminated many of the insights discussed in this work.

As a result of these experiences, my scholarship has come to focus specifically on the role of ethics in the study of games as it has evolved over the last twenty years. Using my research as a basis for discussion, I trace the path of games as a medium of communication and its increased datafication as well as what that has meant for game design, players, and developers. Looking into the future, the data used to train machine learning algorithms for games specifically and necessarily must coincide with an increase in the role of ethics, privacy, and policy expertise in the co-constitution of our shared extended realities.

Anthropologist Clifford Geertz (2000/1983) is known for stating "a scholar can hardly be better employed than in destroying a fear." No more vividly is this sentiment realized than in the public discourse surrounding the irrational fear and misunderstanding of new forms of media, especially online games. In my work, I have pursued my research as both an individual and collective pursuit. Individually, I have sought out cultures and everyday lives that may shed light upon the role played by online games in our society. Collectively, I have used these findings toward teachable moments that demystify the losses and gains afforded by new forms of media. Accordingly, I regard the work here as a rejection of the construction of online games as a problem eliciting moral panic associated with online games that are all too ubiquitous in mainstream media.

Rather than oversimplifying a heightened level of engagement with online games and gaming, there are many reasons people play games in Korea. It is not enough to call the Korean phenomenon "addiction." Rather, online games in this sense are a medium of cultural communication, and part of an intricate system of culture, society, politics, and economics, as exemplified with cases in Chee and Karhulahti (2020). I have been concerned with the tangible world that surrounds "virtual" ones, and how those worlds exist in symbiotic dialogue with one another. That is, rather than being concerned with life "behind" the screen, I argued for the perspective that the lives surrounding those screens are indeed social and intersubjective (Chee et al., 2006). It is through this constant reminder that I have conducted this study of communication media in a cultural context.

My research presented an atypical critique of the typically celebratory and/or panicked tenor associated with technological adoption in Korea. Reports that clearly laud the rapid uptake of ICTs in Korea, citing forward-looking policies and innovative implementation (Lewis, 2004), have highlighted the online gaming industry and its place in popular culture as an economic strength and path to the nation's future in the global information society (Lee, 2005).

Considering both the positive, negative, and indeterminate outcomes in the case of Korean online gaming, some have felt compelled to ask questions to the effect of, "Should the use of online games be regulated?" (Miller, 2002) or "Does this case show how society shapes technology, or vice versa?" (Feenberg and Bakardjieva, 2004) or even, "Can Korea's case of policy and ICTs be used as a model for other countries in how cultures receive and appropriate technologies?" (Ho, 2005). My questions have been considerably simpler, but the answers are more complex.

As stated in my introduction, the three primary questions driving my inquiry have been:

1. What factors have contributed to the prominence of online gaming culture in contemporary Korea?
2. How have online games played a role as a communication medium?
3. How has the Figure of gaming interacted with the Ground of a local context such as Korea's?

In particular, I wished to look at the relationship between various social pressures experienced by Korean youth in their everyday life, and their media use. I argued that these relationships do not exist independently from culture, social structure, and infrastructure but are rather facilitated by such. My goal has been to build an increased understanding of cultural factors specific to Korea in the evaluation and implementation of technology and its associated societal consequences. Furthermore, I attempted to link the government policy initiatives, industrial relationships, and social history that, I argue, have been instrumental in driving the frenetic pace of technology use-culture in contemporary Korea.

Games are receiving an ever-increasing amount of attention in the media and the academe. It has given me a sense of purpose to create a project that documented how games as a medium of communication arose from information infrastructural initiatives. Such a path is a repeat as we have seen with the Minitel (Feenberg, 1995), where an information-based initiative truly caught on in popular use only when it became a way people could communicate and socialize. In this study of Korean sociotechnical transformation, I have given a comprehensive analysis of what gave rise to online gaming in Korea, how it is employed in mainstream youth practices, and why some of those same youth continue to be involved in the games industry as they make careers for themselves.

I felt that I went to Korea being relatively sure what the motivations of those who run Internet Addiction centers were. I was also quite certain about why professional gamers pursued their activities everyday with fervor. The nature of my puzzlement and main preoccupation was how users (the so-called addicts and self-professed gamers) made sense of their world. How did they come into gaming, and what were their motivations? If I lived in Korea, participated in and observed the culture, would I end up having similar motivations, or at the very least understand those motivations?

## THE REMIX SOCIETY

The goal of this book is ultimately to be of service to those who have been underserved by virtue of their participation in community through games and play. Those who have had special disservice done to them by inaccurate and sensationalist media representations, racial stereotyping, or marginalization through gender and sexuality have been too often lumped into the gamer identity, and subsequently scapegoated. I temper the debates surrounding online games addiction by considering how the sociopolitical and economic imperatives of global society have manifested, particularly in the Korean cultural milieu. My keenly insightful informants, as well as intensive ethnographic fieldwork have driven the insights here. In my research, I have looked at technology and society through the lens of Kenneth Burke's "Definition of Man" in *Professing the New Rhetorics* (Burke, 1994, pp. 53–54):

> Man is the symbol-using (symbol making, symbol misusing) animal, inventor of the negative, separated from his natural condition by instruments of his own making, goaded by the spirit of hierarchy (or moved by the sense of order), and rotten with perfection.

As technology is a symbol of many things (including progress, modernity, transcendence, emancipation, etc.) it is especially helpful to view it as such during my study of Korean phenomena during my time there. Formidable scholars like Nancy Abelmann have presented arguments both accordant and discordant with the Korean tendency to view things in dichotomous relations. The diasporic conditions in which contemporary Koreans find themselves, along with the Neo-Confucian hierarchical social structure also played a part in my investigation.

Through the limited amount of evidence I presented here, I wished to act as a curator, letting the qualitative data provide evocative imagery and easing some clarity out from under the cacophony of situated fieldwork. Ultimately, the aim of conducting years of research on this topic was to question whether or not the aforementioned types of questions are appropriate in this particularly complex situation that brings together media and user-related issues, but also the implementation of the policies and visions of key players from the government and industrial sectors in addressing the prevalence of online gaming culture in Korea.

To date, much of the discussion about online games addiction has centered on psychological models of diagnosis (Miller, 1995; Skinner, 1974) to the "addictiveness" or persuasion of the game or in-game elements in and of itself (Turkle, 1995). If there has been discussion of social/offline consequences of gameplay, it has primarily been framed within studies concerned with negative media-effects that paint users as passive consumers, or the media as existing in isolation of a cultural milieu (Poole, 2000; Wolf, 2001). I have referenced countless studies on new media use that take our current understanding of media use and addiction for granted, with little or no critique of the foundations of that understanding, a problematic aspect which I attempt to highlight in my work. On the bright side, there is an increasing body of literature that does address various externalities to the relations users have with particular media, though they continue to be on the margins compared to dominant paradigms of understanding of media use in these fields.

It was my intention to throw the meanings of diagnosis, regulation, and cultural value of excessive game playing into question by doing an in-depth examination into the context of Korean online game culture. My analysis of cultural determinants of online game use in Korea brought together a number of disciplinary lenses in order to lift restrictions on aspects of events that clarify and lend context to assertions that have been made in other studies of games and their addicted players. Meyrowitz hailed from studies in microsociology. Scholars like Erving Goffman (1959) emphasized dramaturgy and viewed the world as a stage. McLuhan's project has been similar to Goffman's, except his theoretical treatment focused on the human as opposed to theater. Though it would not have been possible forty years ago, we are at an academic moment in time that necessitates the merging of traditions and perspectives to understand new forms of media like online games. As we work to understand how technologies interact with society, it is all the more important to realize how new media might not be that new after all.

Some social phenomena simply require someone to draw attention to what everyday actors in a situation have, in McLuhan's terms, become too numb to see for themselves or even think their actions to be culturally significant at all. He refers to Werner Heisenberg, in *The Physicist's Conception of Nature*, who points out that "technical change alters not only habits of life, but patterns of thought and valuation" (McLuhan, 1994, p. 63). As culture becomes retribalized, "tribal cultures cannot entertain the possibility of the individual or of the separate citizen. Their ideas of spaces and times are neither continuous nor uniform, but compassional and compressional in their intensity" (McLuhan, 1994, p. 84). Indeed, implicit in McLuhan's rumination is the re-emergence of a necessity to assess kinship and interdependence as cornerstones of communication.

The way games have manifested in Korean culture is very much a McLuhanesque picture in how this medium has extended the self, and as a result extended people's possibilities. In McLuhan's discussion of retribalization, he notes a marked difference in speed of actions in the mechanical age with the actions in the present (at the time) electric age. "Slow movement ensured that the reactions were delayed for considerable periods of time. Today the action and the reaction occur almost at the same time. We actually live mythically and integrally, as it were, but we continue to think in the old, fragmented space and time patterns of the pre-electric age" (McLuhan, 1994, p. 4). With the instantaneous speed at which those with access to high-speed networks can conduct their everyday lives, we are seeing a simultaneous "warming" of hot and cool media, which has implications for how we examine in media studies, and with which methodological paradigms.

## SNAPSHOTS IN TIME

The original work upon which this book and collaborations have been based has served scholarship in the area regarding the motivations of online gamers. It has been critical of building technology policy and health programs based on the premise of addiction to games in the conventional sense. My approach to this area, to look at everyday life around game communities and the systemic reasons for participation in these forms of engagement, has been a way to show just how much more there is to consider beyond Korea being a "nation of game addicts" warranting sanctions on gameplay. I regard this work as an act of solidarity and love with gamers worldwide. Though I have chosen to focus on a few select moments here that have to do with online game culture in Korea, there is much that has informed the process, deliberately excluded in the interests of creating a streamlined argument. My desire to prevent the pathologization of an activity that brings joy and sociality is what set me on this path more than twenty years ago.

During my stays in-residence in Korea, I conducted a vast number of interviews and conducted studies on topics such as the Korean wireless industry (Hira et al., 2012), the educational environments of children informed and inspired by the work of Stewart (2004) and Grimes (2021), and the role played by games and other technologies. Korean cultural notions of domesticity served to greatly enrich and complicate my perspectives on gaming culture. Through being physically present and engaging in a variety of different activities, I was exposed to Korean culture, values, and emergent practices in an intense and holistic manner that strangely begged me to connect the dots.

Further muddying the waters of an already messy endeavor, I conducted a multinational study of online game culture and the spaces gaming takes place. Beyond Korea, this research took me into the lived realities of gamers in various countries, including Mexico, Japan, Singapore, India, and the United Arab Emirates. The findings and experiences from that study at times aligned with my understanding of Korean gaming culture, at other times it was completely turned on its head. I was very conflicted about whether or not to include insights from other countries or even other data gathered while in Korea. Though that study occupied me for more than a year, and the projects that followed in the decade since completing my doctoral studies, I am ultimately pleased with the choice to focus my efforts on a comprehensive examination of Korea in a depth at which I am satisfied for the purposes of this book.

I still have a complicated relationship with the question of where I'm "from" or whether or not folks might call me a "games researcher." These assignments make more limitations than they enable. What has unified my research agenda has been its focus on humanity and what makes people tick. To distinguish a twitch from a wink, as Geertz would say.

I did not discuss specific game content or in-game interactions in this work. To do so would have been limiting in that it would have taken away from the examination regarding the transient actions between users and their environments, which is more the topic in which I have always been interested. Indeed, my preoccupation has always been more the form than the content. Still connecting the dots, my current research is focused upon examining the sociocultural contexts of technological engagement and experience, with a particular emphasis on games and social media. Drawing upon my training in applied social science methods and especially anthropological approaches, I have designed and conducted numerous international ethnographic fieldwork studies. Throughout my academic career, my scholarship has centered on the questions surrounding how and why people may be compelled to play games at varying levels and modes of engagement.

This, and other works of mine have been driven by an overarching interest in the place and meaning of online games in everyday life. Given that this book has explored what games mean in the lives of Korean youth according to the ethnographic data, I examined the factors through which games—as a medium of communication—can be understood within a cultural context. My research agenda stems from a dissatisfaction with conventional explanations for engagement with technology that oversimplify relationships, leaving social aspects woefully underrepresented. Sometimes it is not appropriate to reduce a question concerning society and technology to a simple variable.

In addressing the question of how gaming became mainstream culture in South Korea, the research findings pointed to the country's particular national circumstances, including the porous boundaries between its culture, social structure, infrastructure, and policy factors within an environment of massive sociotechnical upheaval. I am still digesting the ethnographic insights I collected, and given how mobility and transition have been knit into the fabric of Seoul's development, examining the rate of development over the last twenty years continues to capture the imagination of nations in different positions along the developmental scale.

Gaming in the ubiquitous PC bangs has been central to the experience of urban movement, and what an examination of the Korean technoscape implies is a counterversion of publicness in the context of global modernities in the North, South, East, or West. In this sense, technologies have been embedded in the development and how our understanding of culture and technology must accordingly evolve. I am continuing to reach out to other disciplinary persuasions in order to combine and confront the ideas of how digital technologies undermine public space along with the everyday life of youth and their relationship with modernity and corresponding ideas of rights and privacy.

This book illuminated some of the darker, underexamined corners of international games culture by providing one exceptional case, amongst the many exceptional cases worldwide. The ethnographic insights conveyed during the course of this discussion pointed largely to how online games as a medium of communication allowed for the formation and maintenance of community, along with upward mobility and social change in the Korean context. Some nights, it might just be about students finding ways to stay out all night until the subway starts up again.

In this contribution to the global conversation on games, I hope to have provided enough compelling evidence to cause someone to ponder the inherent good or evil of games a little longer.

Insight becomes the light by which we banish the shadows of fear. My work finds itself joining good company now, and in the future of play.

Now, onto bigger and badder monsters in the next quest. Ding!

# Bibliography

Abelmann, N. (2003). The melodrama of mobility: Women, talk, and class in contemporary South Korea. Honolulu: University of Hawaii Press.

Agar, M. (1996). The professional stranger: An informal introduction to ethnography (2nd ed.). San Diego: Academic Press.

Alexander, B. K. (2008). The globalisation of addiction: A study in poverty of the spirit. Oxford; New York: Oxford University Press.

Allen, S. L. (Ed.). (1994). Media anthropology: Informing global citizens. Westport, Conn.: Bergin & Garvey.

Amsden, A. H. (1989). Asia's next giant: South Korea and late industrialization. New York: Oxford University Press.

Anderson, B. (1991). Imagined communities: Reflections on the origin and spread of nationalism (Rev. and extended ed., 2nd ed.). New York: Verso.

Angus, I. H. (2000). Primal scenes of communication: Communication, consumerism, and social movements. Albany: State University of New York Press.

Attallah, P. a. L. R. S. (2002). The institutional context. In P. a. L. R. S. Attallah (Ed.), Mediascapes: New patterns in Canadian communication. Vancouver, CA: Nelson Thompson Learning.

Babe, R. E. (2000). Canadian communication thought: Ten foundational writers. Toronto: University of Toronto Press.

Bakardjieva, M. (2005). Internet society: The internet in everyday life. London: Sage Publications.

Bedeski, R. E. (1983). South Korea's modernization: Confucian and conservative characteristics. Downsview, Ont.: University of Toronto-York University, Joint Centre on Modern East Asia.

Bedeski, R. E. (1994). The transformation of South Korea. London; New York: Routledge.

Bell, G. (2006). No more SMS from Jesus: Ubicomp, religion, and techno-spiritual practices. In P. Dourish & A. Friday (Eds.), Ubicomp 2006 (pp. 141–158). Berlin, Heidelberg: Springer-Verlag.

Bergstrom, K. (2009). Introducing "surveylady": A case for the use of avatars as part of gaming research. Stream: Culture/Politics/Technology, 2(1), 18–22.

BHEF. (2010). Increasing the number of STEM graduates: Insights from the U.S. STEM education & modeling project. BHEF.
Biggart, N. W. (1998). Deep finance: The organizational bases of South Korea's financial collapse. Journal of Management Inquiry, 7, 311–320.
Boellstorff, T. (2008). Coming of age in second life: An anthropologist explores the virtually human. Princeton: Princeton University Press.
Bogost, I. (2007). Persuasive games: The expressive power of videogames. Cambridge, Mass.: MIT Press.
Bourdieu, P. (1984). Distinction: A social critique of the judgment of taste (R. Nice Trans.). Henley: Routledge and Kegan Paul.
Buckingham, D. (1997). Electronic child abuse? Rethinking the media's effects on children. In M. Barker & J. Petley (Eds.), Ill effects: The media violence debate (pp. 63–77). London; New York: Routledge.
Burke, K. (1994). Definition of man. In T. Enos, & S. C. Brown (Eds.), Professing the new rhetorics: A sourcebook (pp. 40–62). Englewood Cliffs, NJ: Prentice Hall.
Caillois, R. (1961). Man, play, and games. New York: Free Press.
Cassegard, C. (2001). Murakami haruki and the naturalization of modernity. International Journal of Japanese Sociology, 10.
Castells, M. (2004). The network society. Cheltenham, UK; Northampton, Mass.: Edward Elgar Pub.
Castronova, E. (2005). Synthetic worlds: The business and culture of online games. Chicago: University of Chicago Press.
Chee, F. (2006). The games we play online and offline: Making wang-tta in Korea. Popular Communication, 4(3), 225–239.
Chee, F. (2016). A game industry beyond diversity: systemic barriers to participation in South Korea. In Y. Kafai, G. Richard, & B. Tynes (Eds). Diversifying Barbie and Mortal Kombat: Intersectional perspectives and inclusive designs in gaming (pp. 159–170). Carnegie Mellon University ETC Press.
Chee, F., de Castell, S., & Taylor, N. (2011). Public virtual world gaming in Asia: Preparatory fieldwork for site selection, protocol testing and research instrument development. Simon Fraser University Library.
Chee, F., Hjorth, L. & Davies, H. (2021). An ethnographic co-design approach to promoting diversity in the games industry. Feminist Media Studies. doi:10.1080/1 4680777.2021.1905680
Chee, F., and Karhulahti, V.-M. (2020). "The ethical and political contours of Institutional Promotion in eSports: from precariat models to sustainable practices." Human Technology, Open Science Centre, 16(2). doi: https://doi.org/10.17011/ht/ urn.202008245642
Chee, F., and Smith, R. (2003). Is electronic community an addictive substance? Level Up: Digital Games Research Conference, Utrecht, The Netherlands.
Chee, F., & Smith, R. (2005). Is electronic community an addictive substance? An ethnographic offering from the EverQuest community. In S. P. Schaffer, & M. L. Price (Eds.), Interactive convergence: Critical issues in multimedia (pp. 137–155). Oxford, UK: Inter-Disciplinary Press.

Chen, M. G. (2009). Communication, coordination, and camaraderie in world of warcraft. Games and Culture, 4(1), 47–73. doi:10.1177/1555412008325478

Chess, Shira. (2017). Ready player two: women gamers and designed identity. University of Minnesota Press.

Chung, Peichi. (2021). Introduction to part III. In M. Lee & P. Chung (Eds.), Media technologies for work and play in East Asia (pp. 199–204). https://doi.org/10.46692/9781529213386.012

Chung, Peichi. (2008). New media for social change: Globalization and the online gaming industries of South Korea and Singapore. Science, Technology, & Society (New Delhi, India), 13(2), 303–323. https://doi.org/10.1177/097172180801300207

Clark, N., & Scott, P. S. (2009). Game addiction: The experience and the effects. Jefferson, N.C.: McFarland.

Clifford, J., Marcus, G. E., & School of American Research. (1986). Writing culture: The poetics and politics of ethnography: A School of American Research advanced seminar. Berkeley: University of California Press.

Confucius. (1979). The analects (D. C. Lau Trans.). London: Penguin Books.

Conger, C. (2011, November 4). Don't blame Facebook for the narcissism epidemic. Discovery News.

Consalvo, M. (2016). Atari to Zelda: Japan's videogames in global contexts. The MIT Press.

Consalvo, M. (2007). Cheating: Gaining advantage in videogames. Cambridge, Mass.: Massachusetts Institute of Technology.

Consalvo, M., & Paasonen, S. (2002). Women & everyday uses of the internet: Agency & identity. New York: Peter Lang.

Cote, Amanda. (2021). Gaming sexism: gender and identity in the era of casual video games. New York University Press.

Czitrom, D. J. (1982). Media and the American mind: From Morse to McLuhan. Chapel Hill: University of North Carolina Press.

de Castell, S., & Jenson, J. (2007). Worlds in play: International perspectives on digital games research. New York: Peter Lang.

de Freitas, S., & Griffiths, M. (2008). The convergence of gaming practices with other media forms: What potential for learning? A review of the literature. Learning, Media and Technology, 33(1), 11–20. doi:10.1080/17439880701868796.

Debord, G. (1983). Society of the spectacle. Detroit: Black & Red.

Desai, R. A., Krishnan-Sarin, S., Cavallo, D., & Potenza, M. N. (2010). Video-gaming among high school students: Health correlates, gender differences, and problematic gaming. Pediatrics, 126(6), e1414–e1424. doi:10.1542/peds.2009-2706.

Dibbell, J. (1998). My tiny life: Crime and passion in a virtual world (1st ed.). New York: Holt.

Dogakinai, A. (1999). Ijime: A social illness of Japan. Portland, Ore.: Lewis Clark College.

Dourish, P., & Bell, G. (2011). Divining a digital future: Mess and mythology in ubiquitous computing. Cambridge, Mass.: MIT Press.

Dovey, J., & Kennedy, H. W. (2006). Game cultures: Computer games as new media. Maidenhead, Berkshire, England; New York, NY: Open University Press.

Dyer-Witheford, N., & De Peuter, G. (2009). Games of empire: Global capitalism and video games. Minneapolis: University of Minnesota Press.

Evans-Pritchard, E. E. (1971/1940). The nuer: A description of the modes of livelihood and political institution of a nilotic people. Oxford, Eng.: Clarendon Press, 1940, 1971 printing.

Fackler, M. (2007, November 18). In Korea, a boot camp cure for web obsession. New York Times.

Federal Trade Commission Consumer Alert 38. Virtual worlds and kids: Mapping the risks. Retrieved from http://www.ftc.gov/bcp/edu/pubs/consumer/alerts/alt038.shtm

Feenberg, A. (1995). Alternative modernity: The technical turn in philosophy and social theory. Berkeley, California: University of California Press.

Feenberg, A. (1999). Questioning technology. London: Routledge.

Feenberg, A., & Bakardjieva, M. (2004). Virtual community: No "killer implication." New Media & Society, 6(1), 37–43.

Fickle, T. (2020). The race card: from gaming technologies to model minorities. New York University Press.

Franklin, U. (1999). The real world of technology. Toronto: Anansi.

Funk, J. (2012, July 6). Flash game makes players beat up "tropes vs. women" creator. Message posted to http://www.escapistmagazine.com/news/view/118310-Flash-Game-Makes-Players-Beat-Up-Trop es-vs-Women-Creator

Galloway, A. R. (2004). Protocol. Cambridge, Mass.: MIT Press.

Geartest.com, S. (2004). Living the dream: Life as a professional gamer. Geartest.com.

Geertz, C. (1973). The interpretation of cultures: Selected essays. New York: Basic Books.

Geertz, C. (2000). Available light: Anthropological reflections on philosophical topics. Princeton, N.J.: Princeton University Press.

Geertz, C. (2000/1983). Available light: Anthropological reflections on philosophical topics. Princeton, N.J.: Princeton University Press.

Gluck, C. (2002). South Korea's gaming addicts. BBC News.

Goffman, E. (1959). The presentation of self in everyday life. Garden City, N.Y.: Doubleday.

Gray, K. (2020). Intersectional tech: Black users in digital gaming. Baton Rouge: Louisiana State University Press.

Greenfield, A. (2006). Everyware: The dawning age of ubiquitous computing. Berkeley, Calif.: New Riders.

Griffiths, M.D., Davies, M.N.O., & Chappell, D. (2003). Breaking the stereotype: The case of online gaming. CyberPsychology & Behavior, 6(1), 81–91.

Grimes, S. (2021). Digital playgrounds: The hidden politics of children's online play spaces, virtual worlds, and connected games. Toronto: University of Toronto Press.

Gubrium, J. F., & Holstein, J. A. (2002). Handbook of interview research. Thousand Oaks, Calif.; London: Sage.

Gusfield, J. R. (1996). Contested meanings: The construction of alcohol problems. Madison: The University of Wisconsin Press.

Halavais, A. (2006). Cyberporn and society. Dubuque, IA: Kendall/Hunt.

Haraway, D. J. (1991). Simians, cyborgs, and women: The reinvention of nature. London: Free Association Books.

Hira, A., Morfopolous, J., & Chee, F. (2012). Evolution of the South Korean wireless industry: From state guidance to global competition. International Journal of Technology and Globalisation, 1(2), 65–86.

Hjorth, L. (2006). Playing at being mobile: Gaming and cute culture in South Korea. Fibreculture, (8).

Hjorth, L. (2011). Games and gaming: An introduction to new media. Oxford: Berg.

Hjorth, L., & Chan, D. (2009). Gaming cultures and place in Asia-Pacific. New York; London: Routledge.

Ho, A. (2005, Mar 18). Broadband: Virtually a den of iniquity? The Straits Times, p. 27.

Hofstede, G. H. (1997). Cultures and organizations: Software of the mind (Rev ed.). New York: McGraw-Hill.

Hong, G. (2004). Emotions in culturally-constituted relational worlds. Culture and Psychology, 10(1), 53–63.

Huizinga, J. (1955). Homo ludens: A study of the play element in culture. Boston: The Beacon Press.

Itō, M. (2009). Engineering play: A cultural history of children's software. Cambridge, Mass.: MIT Press.

Jenkins, H. (2006). Convergence culture: Where old and new media collide. New York: New York University Press.

Jin, D. Y. (2010). Korea's online gaming empire. Cambridge, Mass.: MIT Press.

Jin, D. Y. (2011). Hands on hands off: The Korean state and the market liberalization of the communication industry (1st ed.). New York, NY: Hampton Press.

Jin, D. Y., & Chee, F. (2008). Age of new media empires: A critical interpretation of the Korean online game industry. Games and Culture: A Journal of Interactive Media, 3(1), 58.

Jonsson, F. (2010). A public place of their own. A fieldstudy of a game café as a Third Place. Proceedings of DiGRA Nordic, Experiencing Games: Games, Play, and Players.

Jouhki, J. (2008). Korean communication and mass media research: Negotiating the west's influence. International Journal of Communication, 2, 23.

Katz, J. E. (2006). Magic in the air: Mobile communication and the transformation of social life. New Brunswick, NJ: Transaction Publishers.

Kendall, L. (2002). Hanging out in the virtual pub: Masculinities and relationships online. Berkeley, CA: University of California Press.

Kim, J. H., Lee, Y. M., Kim, M. G., & Kim, E. J. (2006). A study on the factors and types of on-line game addiction: An application of the self-determination theory. Journal of Korean Communication, 50(5), 79–107.

Kim, P. (2011). Contextualizing the ideas of technology in Korea—questions of technology and early modern experiences. Technology in Society, 33, 52–58.

Kim, T. (2005). Internet addiction haunts Korea. Seoul: The Korea Times.

Kline, S., Dyer-Witheford, N., & de Peuter, G. (2003). Digital play: The interaction of technology, culture, and marketing. Montréal: McGill-Queen's University Press.

Kondo, D. K. (1990). Crafting selves: Power, gender, and discourses of identity in a Japanese workplace. Chicago: University of Chicago Press.

Larson, J. F. (1995). The telecommunications revolution in Korea. Hong Kong; New York: Oxford University Press.

Latour, B. (1993). We have never been modern (C. Porter Trans.). London: Harvester Wheatsheaf.

Lee, A. J. (2005). e-Sports as a growing industry. (No. 20). Seoul, Korea: Samsung Economic Research Institute.

Lee, K. J. (2002, January 29). Game Market watches PS2. Financial News.

Lewis, P. (2004, September 20). South Korea: Broadband wonderland. Fortune Magazine.

Lie, J. (1998). Han Unbound: The political economy of South Korea. Stanford, Calif.: Stanford University Press.

Lindtner, S., & Szablewicz, M. (2011). China's many internets: Participation and digital game play across a changing technology landscape. In D. K. Herold, & P. Marolt (Eds.), Online society in China: Creating, celebrating, and instrumentalising the online carnival (pp. 89–105). Abingdon, Oxon; New York: Routledge.

Malaby, T. (2006). Parlaying value: Capital in and beyond virtual worlds. Games and Culture, 1(2), 141–162.

Malinowski, B. (1964). Argonauts of the western Pacific: An account of native enterprise and adventure in the archipelagoes of Melanesian New Guinea. London: Routledge and Sons, Ltd.

Malinowski, B. (1967). A diary in the strict sense of the term. New York: Harcourt, Brace and World.

Marcus, G. E. (1998). Ethnography through thick and thin. Princeton, NJ: Princeton University Press.

McGonigal, J. (2011). Reality is broken: Why games make us better and how they can change the world. New York: Penguin Press.

McLuhan, M. (1994). Understanding media: The extensions of man. Boston: The MIT Press.

McLuhan, M., & McLuhan, E. (1988). Laws of media: The new science. Toronto: University of Toronto Press.

McLuhan, M., Staines, D., & McLuhan, S. (2003). Understanding me: Lectures and interviews. Toronto: McClelland & Stewart.

Menzies, H. (1996). Whose brave new world? The information highway and the new economy. Toronto: Between the Lines.

Meyrowitz, J. (1985). No sense of place: The impact of electronic media on social behavior. New York: Oxford University Press.

Miller, D., & Slater, D. (2000). The Internet: An ethnographic approach. Oxford: Berg.

Miller, N. S. (1995). Addiction psychiatry: Current diagnosis and treatment. N.Y.: Wiley-Liss.

Miller, S. A., II. (2002, March 31). Death of a game addict. Milwaukee Journal Sentinel.
Mosco, V. (2004). The digital sublime: Myth, power, and cyberspace. Cambridge, Mass.: MIT Press.
Nahm, A. (1993). Introduction to Korean history and culture = sin han'guksa immun. Elizabeth, N.J.: Hollym.
Nakamura, L. (2002). Cybertypes: race, ethnicity, and identity on the Internet. N.Y.: Routledge.
Nakamura, L. (2008). Digitizing race: Visual cultures of the internet. Minneapolis: University of Minnesota Press.
Nardi, B. (2010). My life as a night elf priest: An anthropological account of world of warcraft. Ann Arbor: University of Michigan Press: University of Michigan Library.
Nardi, B., & Miller, J. (1990). An ethnographic study of distributed problem solving in spreadsheet development. Palo Alto, Calif.: Hewlett-Packard Laboratories.
Negroponte, N. (1995). Being digital. London: Hodder & Stoughton.
Nietzsche, F. (1989). On the genealogy of morals and ecce homo (W. Kaufmann Trans.). Random House.
Oh, M., & Larson, J. F. (2011). Digital development in Korea: Building an information society. Abingdon, Oxon; New York: Routledge.
Oh, M., & Larson, J. F. (2020). Digital development in Korea: Building an information society (2nd ed.). Abingdon, Oxon; New York: Routledge.
Oldenburg, R. (1997). The great good place. New York: Marlowe and Company.
Onufrijchuk, R. (1993). "Introducing Innis/McLuhan concluding: The Innis in McLuhan's 'system.'" Continuum: The Australian Journal of Media & Culture, 7(1).
Onufrijchuk, R. (1998). Object as vortex: Marshall McLuhan & material culture as media of communication. Burnaby: Simon Fraser University.
Orr, J. E. (1996). Talking about machines: An ethnography of a modern job. Ithaca, N.Y.: Cornell University Press.
Padgett, D. K. (2003). Coming of age: Theoretical thinking, social responsibility, and global perspective in qualitative research. In D. K. Padgett (Ed.), The qualitative research experience (pp. 297–315). Belmont, Calif.: Wadsworth.
Paul, C. (2020). Free-to-Play: Mobile video games, bias, and norms. Cambridge, Mass.: MIT Press.
Pearce, C., Boellstorff, T., & Nardi, B. (2009). Communities of play: Emergent cultures in multiplayer games and virtual worlds. Cambridge, Mass.: MIT Press.
Peele, S. (1989). Diseasing of America: Addiction treatment out of control. Lexington, Mass.: Lexington Books.
Pew Research Center. (2010). Millennials: A portrait of generation next. Pew Research Center.
Poole, S. (2000). Trigger happy: The inner life of videogames. London: Fourth Estate.
Postman, N. (1985). Amusing ourselves to death: Public discourse in the age of show business. New York: Viking.

Prey, R. (2005). How do you say "imperialism"? The English language teaching industry and the culture of imperialism in South Korea. Burnaby, B.C.: Simon Fraser University.

Pricewaterhouse Coopers. (2006). Global entertainment and media outlook 2006–2010.

Pricewaterhouse Coopers. (2007). Global entertainment and media outlook 2007–2011.

Pricewaterhouse Coopers. (2008). Global entertainment and media outlook 2008–2012.

Putnam, R. D. (2000). Bowling alone: The collapse and revival of American community. New York: Simon & Schuster.

Rapping, E. (Ed.). (2000). U.S. talk shows, feminism, and the discourse of addiction. N.J.: Hampton Press Inc.

Republic of South Korea. (2001). Public Performance Act, Law Viewer. https://elaw.klri.re.kr/eng_mobile/viewer.do?hseq=55269&type=part&key=17

Rheingold, H. (2002). Smart mobs: The next social revolution. Cambridge, Mass.: Perseus Publishing.

Royse, P., Lee, J., Undrahbuyan, B., Hopson, M., & Consalvo, M. (2007). Women and games: Technologies of the gendered self. New Media & Society, 9(4), 555–576.

Schaler, J. (2000). Addiction is a choice. Peru, Ill.: Open Court Publishing.

Schutz, A. (1962/1966). Collected papers. The Hague: M. Nijhoff.

Schutz, A. (1970). On phenomenology and social relations; selected writings. Chicago: University of Chicago Press.

Seay, F., & Kraut, R. (2007). Project massive: Self-regulation and problematic use of online gaming. Proceedings ACM Conference on Human Factors in Computing Systems, 829–838.

Seth, M. J. (2002). Education fever: Society, politics, and the pursuit of schooling in South Korea. Honolulu: University of Hawai'i Press and Center for Korean Studies, University of Hawai'i.

Simon, B. (2007). Never playing alone: The social contextures of digital gaming. Loading . . . , 1(1). Retrieved from http://journals.sfu.ca/loading/index.php/loading/article/view/20/3

Skinner, B. F. (1974). About behaviorism. New York: Alfred A. Knopf.

Steinkuehler, C. A., & Williams, D. (2006). Where everybody knows your (screen) name: Online games as "Third places." N.J.: Blackwell Publishing Inc.

Stewart, K. (2004). Informatization of a nation: A case study of South Korea's computer gaming and PC-bang culture. (Master's thesis, Simon Fraser University). Master of Arts, 206.

Sutton-Smith, B. (1997). The ambiguity of play. Cambridge, Mass.: Harvard University Press.

Szablewicz. (2010). The ill effects of "opium for the spirit": A critical cultural analysis of China's Internet addiction moral panic. Chinese Journal of Communication, 3(4), 453–470. https://doi.org/10.1080/17544750.2010.516579

Taylor, T. L. (2006). Play between worlds: Exploring online game culture. Cambridge, Mass.: MIT Press.

Taylor, T. L. (2012). Raising the stakes: e-Sports and the professionalization of computer gaming. Cambridge, Mass.: MIT Press.
Taylor, T. L. (2018). Watch me play: Twitch and the rise of game live streaming. Princeton University Press.
Travers, A. (2000). Writing the public in cyberspace: Redefining inclusion on the net. New York: Garland Pub.
Turkle, S. (1995). Life on the screen: Identity in the age of the internet. New York: Simon & Schuster.
Turkle, S. (2011). Alone together: Why we expect more from technology and less from each other. New York: Basic Books.
van Schie, E.G.M. & Wiegman, O. (1997). Children and videogames: Leisure activities, aggression, social integration, and school performance. Journal of Applied Social Psychology, 27(13), 1175–1194.
Wakeford, N. (2003). The embedding of local culture in global communication: Independent internet cafés in London. New Media & Society, 5(3), 379–399. doi:10.1177/14614448030053005.
Wellman, B., & Gulia, M. (1999). Net-surfers don't ride alone: Virtual communities as communities. In B. Wellman (Ed.), Networks in the global village: Life in contemporary communities (pp. 331–366). Boulder, Colo.; Oxford: Westview Press.
Whang, L. S. (2003). Online game dynamics in Korean society: Experiences and lifestyles in the online game world. Korea Journal, Autumn 2003, 7–34.
Wilkinson, N., Ang, R. P., & Goh, D. H. (2008). Online video game therapy for mental health concerns: A review. International Journal of Social Psychiatry, 54(4), 370–382. doi:10.1177/0020764008091659.
Williams, R. (1974). Television: Technology and cultural form. London: Fontana.
Wolf, G. (1996). Channeling McLuhan: The Wired interview with the magazine's patron saint. Wired Magazine, 4(1).
Wolf, M. J. P. (Ed.). (2001). The medium of the video game. Austin: University of Texas Press.
Woo-Cumings, M. (2001). Miracle as prologue: The state and the reform of the corporate sector in Korea. In J. E. Stiglitz, & S. Yusuf (Eds.), Rethinking the East Asian miracle (pp. 343–377). Washington, D.C.; New York: World Bank; Oxford University Press.
Yoon, J. (2011). "Online game shutdown proves controversial." The Korea Times. Retrieved from https://www.koreatimes.co.kr/www/tech/2022/06/133_85847.html
Yoon, K. (2006). The making of Neo-Confucian Cyberkids: Representations of young mobile phone users in South Korea. New Media & Society, 8(5), 753–771.
Yoshimi, Y., & O'Brien, S. (2000). Comfort women: Sexual slavery in the Japanese military during World War II [Jūgun ianfu.]. New York: Columbia University Press.
Young, K. S., & de Abreu, C. N. (2011). Internet addiction: A handbook and guide to evaluation and treatment. Hoboken, N.J.: John Wiley & Sons.
Zimmer, M. (2010). "But the data is already public": On the ethics of research in Facebook. Ethics and Information Technology, 12(4), 313–325.

# Index

Abelmann, Nancy, 28, 30, 104
Academy of Korean Studies, 32
addiction, 3–4, 19, 22, 49, 54, 70, 77, 82–83, 101–106
Agar, Michael, 17
Aion, 64
Alexander, Bruce, 4, 21–22
Amsden, Alice, 27
Anderson, Benedict, 11, 35
Ang, Rebecca P., 21
Angus, Ian, 7
anomie, 7
AOL, 86
Asian Financial Crisis, 29, 36, 80, 89
Association of Internet Researchers (AoIR), 62
Attallah, Paul, 55
Augustine, Saint, 6

Babe, Robert, 6
Bakardjieva, Maria, 11, 64, 102
Bedeski, Robert, 28, 30, 32–34, 43, 75
Bell, Genevieve, 18–19, 70
Bergstrom, Kelly, 14
Biggart, Nicole Woolsey, 42
Blizzard Entertainment, ix
Boellstorff, Tom, 3, 22
Bogost, Ian, 20
Bourdieu, Pierre, 55

Buckingham, David, 5
Burke, Kenneth, 104

Caillois, Roger, 74
Cassegard, Carl, 28
Castells, Manuel, 28
Castronova, Edward, 22
Cavallo, Dana A., 21
chaebol, 43, 82, 85, 97, 100
chae myun, 72–73
Chan, Dean, 45, 55
Chappell, Darren, 21
Chee, Florence, 2, 12–13, 15, 21, 27, 30, 38, 44–45, 55, 60, 63–65, 70, 73, 87, 102, 106
Chen, Mark, 21
Chess, Shira, 94
Chung, Peichi, 59
Clark, Neils, 9, 22, 61
Clifford, James, 17
Confucius, 30, 33–37
Consalvo, Mia, 22, 75, 90
Cote, Amanda, 90
counter-irritant, 2, 65
couple zones, 70
COVID-19, 9
Cyworld, 57, 64
Czitrom, Daniel, 7

Daewoo Corporation, 43
Davies, Hugh, 15, 60
Davies, Mark N. O., 21
de Abreu, Christiano Nabuco, 21–22
de Castell, Suzanne, 22, 65
de Freitas, Sara, 21
de Peuter, Greig, 5, 21
Debord, Guy, 20
Deleuze, Gilles, 27
Demilitarized Zone (DMZ), 32
Desai, Rani A., 21
Dibbell, Julian, 22
Dokdo, 32
Dourish, Paul, 18–19, 70
Dovey, Jon, 3, 22
Dyer-Witheford, Nick, 5, 21

eSports, 20, 50, 56, 71
ethics, 16, 90, 101
ethnographic, 11, 17, 19, 107
Evans-Pritchard, Edward Evan, 18
EverQuest, 2, 22
everyday life, ix, 2, 107

Facebook, 65
Fackler, Martin, 63
Federal Trade Commission (FTC), 23n4
Feenberg, Andrew, 11, 17, 28, 59, 64, 102–103
Fickle, Tara, 90
figure and ground. *See* McLuhan, Marshall
Finnish Museum of Games, 75
first-person shooter (FPS) games, 67
Franklin, Ursula, 21, 62
Funk, John, 95

Galloway, Alexander R., 27
Geertz, Clifford, 5, 16–18, 101, 107
gender, 15, 47, 75, 81, 90, 95–100, 103
global village. *See* McLuhan, Marshall
Goffman, Erving, 105
Goh, Dion H., 21
Gore, Al, 64
GoStop, 65

Greenfield, Adam, 19
Griffiths, Mark, 21
Grimes, Sarah, 106
Gubrium, Jaber F., 14
Gulia, Milena, 17, 64
Gusfield, Joseph R., 19

hagwon, 44, 46
Halavais, Alex, 50
Hangame, 51
Hangul, 39–40
Haraway, Donna, 18
Heisenberg, Werner, 18, 105
Hira, Anil, 27, 38, 106
HiTel, 86
Hjorth, Larissa, 15, 21, 45, 55, 60, 63, 65, 75
Ho, A., 102
Hofstede, Geert, 72
Holstein, James A., 1
Hong, Gui-Young, 33–35
Hopson, Mark, 90
hot and cool media, 10. *See also* McLuhan, Marshall
Huizinga, Johan, 73–74
Hyundai Corporation, 27, 29, 43, 85

IMF Crisis, 29, 42–43, 87–88, 90, 99
Imperial Japan, 38, 40
Information and Communications Technology (ICT), 40
Innis, Harold, 7
Intel Corporation, 19
Itembay, 9
Ito, Mizuko, 22

Jenkins, Henry, 10
Jenson, Jennifer, 22
Jin, Dal Yong, 13, 20–21, 29–30, 42, 44–45, 48, 55, 63, 87
Jonsson, Fatima, 66
Jouhki, Jukka, 63

Karhulahti, Veli-Matti, 102
KartRider, 69–70

Katz, James, 10
Kendall, Lori, 64, 66
Kennedy, Helen W., 3, 22
Kim, Pyungho, 28, 39
Kline, Stephen, 5, 21
Kondo, Dorinne, 15
Korea Telecom, 86
Kraut, Robert, 3
Krishnan-Sarin, Suchitra, 21
kwarosa, 60

Lapham, Lewis, 7
Larson, James, 29, 40–41, 48, 80
Latour, Bruno, 10
Lee, A. J., 102
Lee, Joon, 90
Lewis, Peter, 102
LG Corporation, 27, 29, 42–43, 82
Lindtner, Silvia, 64
Lineage, ix, 31, 64, 69–72

Malaby, Thomas, 22
Malinowski, Bronislaw, 2, 18
Marcus, George, 17
Massachusetts Institute of Technology (MIT), 75
massively multiplayer online role-playing game (MMORPG), 2, 50, 64, 66, 72
McGonigal, Jane, 21
McLuhan, Marshall, 2, 6–8, 55, 57–58, 62–64, 105; figure and ground, 5, 8, 18, 55, 62–63; global village, 61–62; hot and cool media, 10, 105; Narcissus, 57–58, 65; retribalization, 10–11, 18, 60, 105
McLuhan, Stephanie, 6
meaning-making, ix
media, 10, 17
media ecology, 99, 100
Menzies, Heather, 40
Meyrowitz, Joshua, 3, 6, 61, 105
micronarratives, 9
military exemption policy, 47, 90–92

military service, 47, 54, 75–77, 81, 90–92, 100
Miller, Daniel, 11, 17
Miller, Norman S., 104
Miller, S. A., II, 102
Minitel, 103
MMORPG. *See* massively multiplayer online role-playing game
modernity, 10, 104
moral panics, 19, 21, 102
Morfopolous, James, 27, 38, 106
Mosco, Vincent, 27, 40

Nahm, Andrew, 33
Nakamura, Lisa, 18, 22
Narcissus, 57–58. *See also* McLuhan, Marshall
Nardi, Bonnie, 3, 19, 22
National Identification Number (NIN), 49, 68
National Institute for International Education (NIIED), 13
NCSoft, ix, 85, 87
Negroponte, Nicholas, 17
Neo-Confucianism, 33–34, 58, 104
Netflix, 80
NHN Corporation, 81, 89
Nietzsche, Friedrich, 37
NIIED. *See* National Institute for International Education
Nintendo, 32

Oh, Myung, 30, 40–41, 48, 80
Oldenburg, Ray, 64, 66
Onufrijchuk, Roman, 57
Orr, Julian, 19

Paasonen, Susanna, 50, 75
Padgett, Deborah, 21
pandemic, 9
*Parasite*, 80
Park, Chung Hee, 32–33, 41
Patry, Guillaume, 56
Paul, Christopher, 93

PC bang, 5, 13, 23n2, 25–26, 30–31, 40, 44, 50, 54, 56, 59, 66–71, 73, 76–77, 87, 94, 100, 107
Pearce, Celia, 3, 57
Peele, Stanton, 4, 22
Poole, Steven, 104
Postman, Neil, 6, 63
Potenza, Marc N., 21
Prey, Robert, 12
problematic use, 3
pro-gaming. *See* eSports
Public Performance Act, 50, 81
Putnam, Robert, 7, 61, 63

Rapping, Elayne, 22
Real-Time Strategy (RTS) game, 71
retribalization. *See* McLuhan, Marshall
Rheingold, Howard, 17
rhetoric, x
Roh, Moo Hyun, 45, 80
room salons, 97
Royse, Pam, 90

Samsung Corporation, 27, 29, 42–43, 82
Schaler, Jeffrey, 4, 22
school shootings, 9, 23n3
Schutz, Alfred, 64
Scott, Shavaun, 9, 22, 61
Seay, A. Fleming, 3
Seoul National University, 13, 39
Seth, Michael, 38, 45–46
Simon, Bart, 5
Simon Fraser University, 13
Skinner, Burrhus F., 104
Slater, Don, 11, 17
Smith, Richard, 2, 21, 63–64
social networks, 14
Sony Online Entertainment, 22
*Squid Game*, 80
Staines, David, 6
StarCraft, ix, 13, 31, 56, 64, 69, 71–72, 75, 77

status hierarchy, 14, 72, 85, 99
Steinkuehler, Constance, 64, 66
Stewart, Kym, 29, 68
Sutton-Smith, Brian, 11, 62, 69
Szablewicz, Marcella, 64

Takeshima, 32
Taylor, Nicholas, 65
Taylor, T. L., 3, 13, 20, 21–22, 56
techno-fetishists, 3, 22
techno-orientalism, 5, 21–22
Tetris, 75
Travers, Ann, 95
Turkle, Sherry, 6, 17–18, 96, 104

Undrahbuyan, Baasanjav, 90

van Schie, Emil G. M., 21
Vieta, Marcelo, 21, 64

Wakeford, Nina, 44
wang-tta, 72–75
Weber, Max, 5
Wellman, Barry, 17, 64
Whang, Sang-Min, 21
Wiegman, Oene, 21
Wilkinson, Nathan, 21
Williams, Dmitri, 64, 66
Williams, Raymond, 7, 55
Wolf, Mark J., 104
Woo-Cumings, Meredith, 28, 42
World Bank, 28
World of Warcraft, 64, 84, 93

Xerox Corporation, 19

Yoon, Ja-Young, 49
Yoon, Kyongwon, 33, 63
Young, Kimberly, 21–22

Zimmer, Michael, 16

# About the Author

**Florence M. Chee** is associate professor of digital communication in the School of Communication and Program Director of the Center for Digital Ethics and Policy (CDEP) at Loyola University Chicago. She is also Founding Director of the Social & Interactive Media Lab Chicago (SIMLab), devoted to the in-depth study of social phenomena at the intersection of society and technology. Her research examines the social, cultural, and ethical dimensions of emergent digital lifestyles with a particular focus on the examination of artificial intelligence, games, social media, mobile platforms, and translating insights about their lived contexts across industrial, governmental, and academic sectors. She has designed and taught graduate/undergraduate courses in digital media including game studies, where students engage with debates surrounding diversity, intersectionality, and media production through social justice frameworks. Since 2020, she has served as an external consultee to the Freedom Online Coalition's (FOC) Taskforce on Artificial Intelligence and Human Rights (T-FAIR) and is a key constituent of the United Nations 3C Roundtable on Artificial Intelligence. Her first favorite game was Konami's Gyruss (1983), which she played on the Commodore 64.

Ingram Content Group UK Ltd.
Milton Keynes UK
UKHW011301280423
420938UK00004B/19